JUST ANOTHER DAY IN THE
CORPS

KEN LANDRY

PublishAmerica
Baltimore

First printing

ISBN: 1-4137-5897-5
PUBLISHED BY PUBLISHAMERICA, LLLP
www.publishamerica.com
Baltimore

Printed in the United States of America

This book is dedicated to my beautiful wife of 44 years, Masako; to my daughter, Frances, and her husband, Bill; to my son, Brian, and his wife, Kyong; and to my grandchildren, Kendra, Shelby, Nicholas, and Lauren. I would be remiss if I left out my brother-in-law, Bill Oliver. Without his encouraging words and little pep talk along the way, this book would never have been written.

CONTENTS

PREFACE
JULY 27, 1950.

My father and a family friend, Mr. Snow, went with me to downtown NY to the recruiting office as I enlisted in the Marine Corps. Two weeks earlier I had quit my job with the telephone company during my lunch hour, and walked over to Times Square where there was a Navy and Marine Corps recruiting office. The papers that morning were full of stories about the North Koreans invading South Korea and American troops engaging them in battle. I wanted to help! I wanted to fight for my country.

My intention as I approached the recruiting office was to enlist in the Navy. The recruiting office was crowded with men trying to enlist. They all were joining the Navy; only a few guys were standing by the Marine recruiter. Hating to stand in lines, I quickly moved over and stood in front of the desk of a Sgt. in the Marine Corps.

That evening, I dropped the news on my family at the dinner table: I had quit my job and joined the US Marine Corps. You could have heard a pin drop. My older brother said that I was only 18 and could not join without parents' permission. My mom and dad believed him and didn't give it another thought. As far as they were concerned, I wasn't going anywhere. But on a warm sunny day in July, I stood with a group of other young men, ready to go on an adventure that would last a lifetime.

The Major standing at the front of the room warned everyone that if he had any doubts, he should raise his hand now, because the minute we are sworn into the Marine Corps, it would be too late! No one moved and the swearing-in service continued, with the Major finally closing with, "Welcome aboard!"

He told us to say our farewells now because the bus was waiting to take us to Grand Central Station for an overnight trip to Parris Island,

South Carolina. I was about to find out that we were not Marines yet—not by a long shot. The title of "Marine" had to be earned, and the first step to earning the right to be called a Marine was waiting for us…it was called boot camp!

The overnight trip to South Carolina was uneventful. The train stopped at a little town called Beaufort, South Carolina. A porter came through the cars carrying cold Cokes, yelling, "Last chance to get a Coke! Last Chance… Last Chance…" We all joked about it. What did he mean "last chance?"

BOOT CAMP
1950

When the train stopped, a Marine Corporal, with a starched khaki uniform (with not a wrinkle in sight), standing 6'3" tall, with a loud, thunderous voice screamed at us.

"WHEN I TELL YOU TO MOVE, GRAB YOUR F*CKING BAGS AND GET OFF THIS F*CKING TRAIN AND GET ON THAT F*CKING BUS! DON'T OPEN YOUR F*CKING MOUTH, JUST SIT DOWN! MOVE! NOW!"

When the bus came to a stop we were told to get off and fall into formation. We were introduced to our DIs (Drill Instructors), then herded from one building to the next, getting rid of our civilian clothes and donning the Marine Corps utilities. We were also taken to the barber, where in a few seconds, he removed every strand of hair on our heads. Then the endless training began.

Marching, marching, marching...when we were not in class we were marching. They called it "close order drill." And we drilled and drilled and drilled and then drilled some more. And we ran. We were not allowed to walk anywhere. We had to run everywhere, when not in a formation. Parris Island in July is hot. One of the Drill Instructor's favorite thing was to run us around the drill field until we all dropped. He cursed us and called us names, trying everything in his power to break us. The Senior Drill Instructor told us that he would not be happy until all of us were drummed out of the Corps because we couldn't take it. He said that on graduation day he wanted to march down the parade grounds by himself. A lot of the recruits did drop out. Some were sent back to start all over again and some were just sent home.

The meals in the mess hall were okay. The Marines had a rule about food, and there was a large sign stating, "TAKE ALL YOU WANT, BUT EAT ALL YOU TAKE." Well, I mean to tell you, the Marine

Corps means what it says. As we turned our trays in at the end of a meal, they were inspected by a DI and we had best not be throwing any food away. If we did, I guarantee we never did it again. After the meal we had to run back to the barracks and stand at attention outside until the entire platoon had returned. The DIs made sure that we did not waste any time just sitting in the mess hall. They wanted us out and they wanted us out now! That meant that we gulped our food down and took off.

When the entire platoon was assembled after a meal, the DI would yell out the window for the smokers to fall out across the street for a smoke. The smokers even got to sit down and relax. The non-smokers had to stand at attention until the DI called the smokers back to the formation. I quickly became a smoker. It was a habit I kept for my entire Marine Corp career.

When we were issued our rifles, we had to march back to the barracks carrying the rifles in our right hands, just slightly off the ground. One or two Marines dropped their rifles on the way back to the barracks, and they paid for it that night. That afternoon we spent the better part of it learning how to disassemble the weapon and put it back together again. We practiced it over and over and over. The DI had us doing it blindfolded.

This is my Rifle

...There are many like it but this one is mine. My rifle is my best friend. It is my life. I must master it as I master my life.

...My rifle without me is useless. Without my rifle, I am useless. I must fire my rifle true. I must shoot straighter than any of my enemy who is trying to kill me. I must shoot him before he shoots me. I will.

...My rifle and myself know that what counts in this war is not the rounds we fire, the noise of our burst, nor the smoke we make. We know that it is the hits that count. We will.

...My rifle is human, even as I, because it is my life. Thus I will learn it as my brother. I will learn its weakness, its strength, its parts, its accessories, its sights,

and its barrel. I will keep my rifle clean and ready, even as I am clean and ready. We will become part of each other. We will.

...Before God I swear this creed. My rifle and myself are the defender of my country. We are the masters of our enemy. We are the saviors of my life.

...So be it, until victory is America's and there is no enemy but peace...

Every Marine is first and foremost a *rifleman*. The Marine Corps places a strong emphasis on qualifying every year with the rifle. That night at lights out, the two individuals who dropped their rifles on the way back to the barracks slept with them, and not with them assembled, but with all the pieces placed under the mattress cover by the DI, so that which ever way they turned during the night, they would feel the rifle. The DI told them that he would check during the night to make sure they did not remove any of the parts!

The DIs had their own way of putting us to bed. We would stand in our underwear at the foot of our bunk beds, until he yelled, "GET INTO BED, A**HOLES!"

He would then make us get up because we didn't get into our bunks all at the same time. We would go through this routine over and over until he was happy that he could only hear one person jumping into bed...and then silence. We did this every night!

Some nights, when the DI was pissed off at our performance during the day, he would give us a workout before lights out. On command, we would pick up our foot lockers, place them on the top bunk, climb on the bunk with the foot locker, climb down off the top bunk, bring down the footlocker, slide it under the adjacent bottom bunk, crawl after it, and repeat the procedure, from bunk to bunk around the squad bay! When we would get about half way around the squad bay, the DI would scream, "STAND BY YOUR OWN BUNK! NOW!"

Talk about confusion. You have 40 guys with footlockers all trying to get back to their own bunks when your bunk is at the opposite end of the squad bay. Then the DI would go through that get into bed, get out of bed routine. Sleep came quickly.

Getting up in the morning was also an adventure. At 0500 the DI, fully dressed in starched utilities and spit-shined boots, comes in the squad bay, turns on the lights, and shouts, "REVEILLE, REVEILLE, REVEILLE, GET UP, GET UP, GET UP!"

We had to jump out of bed grabbing all our bedding and stand at attention at the foot of the bed. It all happened in a matter of seconds. If we didn't do it fast enough to please him, he had us get back in bed, turn out the lights and do it all over again and again.

We had to make up our bunks the Marine Corps way. They liked the blanket tight so that you could bounce a quarter on the bunk. The DI would go around tearing up bunk after bunk because it was not tight enough. Then it was a mad rush to the head as nature called. After nature's call, you were lucky to get to a sink so that you could see in the mirror. Otherwise you were one of many behind the guy at the sink, and all of you trying to shave. Yes, you had to shave every day whether you needed it or not. If you did not shave and were caught then you dry shaved with a bucket over your head and the DI banging on the bucket with his swagger stick

In the middle of August, Parris Island is *hot*. I remember one day the DI took us back to the barracks, made us close all the windows, then gave us ten minutes to put on *all* of our clothes—I mean every stitch they issued us. Then after having us stand there 'til we were soaking wet with sweat, he would march us around the barracks, stopping us at opposite end of the squad bay. He then told us to remove all the clothing and throw it on the floor in a pile, then get back to our own bunks. With a huge pile of clothes at each end of the squad bay, he then commanded us to retrieve our clothes, place them back in our foot lockers and be ready for inspection in 30 minutes. It was like a sale at a local department store. There was a mad rush to the piles to find our clothes. Collecting them, folding them properly, and putting them back in our foot lockers ready for inspection was a chore. If the clothes weren't marked with your name it would have been impossible.

One of the first items issued to us was the *Marine Corps Guide Book*, the Marine Corps bible. They pounded into our heads the 12 General Orders and every time the DI asked us one or all of them, we were expected to spit it out loud and clear. When we were assigned guard duty, the OD (Officer of the Day) would ask us our general orders as he made his rounds to all the guard posts. If we couldn't answer the

OD, he would reports that back to our DI and our lives would turn into a nightmare! Today, 51 years out of boot camp, I can remember some of them. The words are a little fuzzy but here are a few (not in any special order):

> *...To walk my post in a Military manner keeping always on the alert and observing everything that takes place in sight and hearing.*
> *...To quit my post only when properly relieved.*
> *...To call the Corporal of the Guard in any case not covered by instructions.*
> *...To sound the alarm in case of fire or disorder.*

Being assigned guard duty was a big step for the platoon. The DI drilled it into our heads that standing guard is one of the most important things a Marine can do. When you are on guard in time of war, you have the lives of the fire team, the squad, the platoon, and the entire company in your hands.

I remembered walking my first post and reciting the general orders over and over again aloud while I was walking. I was scared to death that I would forget one of them when the OD (Officer of the Day) inspected the post. When the OD came, he asked me three different General Orders and I was proud as could be because I answered him without hesitation.

One day while on a smoke break, I told a fellow Marine about my hand being sore. I had some kind of an infection around the base of the little finger on my right hand. He told me I should go to sick bay. I didn't know how to go about it going to the sick bay. He told me to request to talk to the DI, so I went into the barracks, knocked on the DI's door, and waited for his roar.

"GET IN HERE...WHAT THE F*CK DO YOU WANT?"

When I told him about my sore hand he went into a rage. He slapped me up against the bulkhead (wall), called me every name in the book (and then some), and kicked me out of his room. I vowed never to ask to go to sick bay again.

My hand got progressively worse and very painful. One day while doing close order drill, the platoon was not making enough noise with our weapons (MI rifles). When we moved our weapons from one position to another position while marching, we were supposed to hit the wooden parts of the stock (wooden body of weapon) with force to make aloud sound.

The DI was very upset with us and made us kneel on the ground and place our rifles on the ground in front of us. Then with the DI calling a marching cadence, we had to slap the ground to make noise.

"HARDER! HARDER!" he yelled.

Well, my right hand was now swollen beyond belief and hurting like hell. I could *not* hit the ground with my right hand. Along came the DI standing right in front of me watching me hit the ground with my left hand and only going through the motion of hitting my right hand on the ground. With one quick movement the DI smashed down on my right hand with his boot. I passed out.

When I opened my eyes, I was in a hospital bed with my right hand bandaged up about the size of a boxing glove. I had been operated on. I had no knowledge of the operation. The doctor later told me that I could have lost some fingers if I waited any longer. To this day my little finger on my right hand is bent and never straightens out. It only bothers me during cold winter days. The skin at the bottom of my little finger was grafted from my left thigh. No one ever asked me what happened!

The problem with going to the hospital during boot camp is that when you go back to boot camp, you have to start over because your platoon has passed you by. Because you grew hair again means another trip to the barber. I was not happy about that. I can't remember how long I was in the hospital, but it was long enough to grow a full head of hair.

When I left the hospital, I was assigned to a new platoon and met my new DIs. I caught a lucky break. The DI, seeing that I had already gone through almost everything, said he would not make me shave my head again. I was to get a short hair cut, but that was better than looking like a skinhead. He also told me that since I had done everything except the rifle range, I would not have to sit through all the classes again. I also was excused from close order drill. When the platoon went to class and/or drill, I was assigned the duty of "fire watch." That meant I remained in the barracks just walking around, making sure everything was secure. I don't know why the DIs were so nice to me!

When it became time for the Rifle Range, we spent the week before learning and practicing, getting into all of the various positions required., which was called "snapping in." It's a very boring time, but it was meant to help us shoot better on the range. It wasn't until much later that I appreciated the "snapping in" period...

The DI had the entire platoon chip in to purchase a portable radio that would go to the highest shooter on qualification day. The highest score one could receive was 250 (50 rounds of ammunition at 5 points per round). We would shoot ten rounds slow fire offhand (standing) at 200 yards, ten rounds rapid fire sitting at 200 yards, ten rounds slow fire kneeling at 300 yards, ten rounds rapid fire prone (lying on the ground) at 300 yards, and ten rounds slow fire prone at 500 yards.

As I said before, all Marines qualify with a rifle every year, because all Marines are first and foremost, riflemen. Of course there could be years when a Marine could not qualify, for various reasons, but in early December 1950, on the range at Paris Island, I not only qualified, but I was the high shooter in the platoon. I felt like I had pitched a no-hitter in the world series or scored the winning touchdown in the Rose Bowl. I was proud as could be as all members of the platoon congratulated me and the even the DI patted me on the back.

After the range, when we arrived back to our original barracks, the DI called me into his room. He again congratulated me and showed me the beautiful radio that the platoon had paid for, that was now mine because I was the high shooter. Then he said that since recruits were not allowed to have a radio, he would hold it for me until after graduation.

A couple of weeks later, it was graduation time. We marched that day like Marine veterans, as proud as could be. We stood tall that day as we listened to all the speakers talking about Marine history and tradition, etc. And with the band playing the "Marine Corps Hymn," we passed in review. We were Marines!

When the DI halted us at the barracks, we waited patiently for the DI to call us Marines for the first time. After a grueling 10-11 weeks of being called shitbirds, maggots, and every other degrading name that you could imagine, we stood waiting and at attention. We roared approval when he bellowed out, "WELL DONE, MARINES! WELCOME TO OUR CORPS!"

Back at the barracks, we turned in all Marine gear, packed up our personal gear, and waited for the DI to pass out our orders to our first duty stations. Mine read, "Camp Lejeune, NC," as did the majority of the platoon's orders. It was time to say good-bye, as we were off on a 12-day leave before we had to report in to our new home. I knocked on the DI's door and asked about my radio. I was told that it dropped and was completely broken and he was sorry …and that was that! At least I got to look at it a couple of weeks earlier. I was a Marine now, and happy to be going home. I was looking forward to what was the beginning of a 20-year adventure.

CAMP LEJEUNE
1950 - 1952 (1ˢᵗ Tour)

Being fresh from boot camp, we were still scared of NCOs (Non-Commissioned Officers) and called everyone we met "sir." It took awhile to get out of that habit. When I checked in for duty, I was assigned to a rifle company. Within the company, I was further assigned to a platoon, then to a squad, then to a fire team. Our platoon sergeant was a crafty old veteran. He yelled a lot and all of us just out of boot camp jumped when he said jump.

I made some good friends in that first platoon. There was Pete M. from Hartford, Connecticut. He was about two or three months ahead of me, so I guess he was considered an "old salt." He talked about his girl continually. On weekends, we often took a trip north to NY, with Pete continuing on to Hartford, Connecticut..

On the base there was a section set aside for Marines who had cars to pick up Marines going in the same direction. It was an orderly system, with a car pulling up and a Military Police officer shouting the destination of the driver. The drivers always wanted x number of dollars for gas. If we agreed, we would head north. For the return trip, I would go to the Washington Bridge toll gates and wait for the ride back. There was always one going back.

In the Marine Corps, you received 30 days of paid leave (vacation) per year. Pete had some time on the books, so he took a ten day leave, went home, and came back married. He was so happy he could hardly control his smiling.

Fate played a trick on Pete though, because he received his orders to go to Korea when he got back to the Corps. He went about two or three months before I did. When I arrived in Korea I tried to find Pete, but found out he was killed his first week there.

Then there was Richard O., a St. Louis guy. He was an administrator (clerk). He was a reservist and had been in for a couple of years . He used to talk about Marines coming back wearing ribbons for Korean service. He always wanted to go but was never called. Richard had a car, A Nash Rambler to be exact. One night on liberty (free time), we drove to Wilmington, NC, about 51 miles from the base. On the way back, Richard said he was tired and asked me to drive back. He never asked if I could drive, and he never asked if I had a license. I didn't volunteer any of that information.

I took the wheel. Lucky for me it was automatic, and off we went. I drove all the way to just outside the base when I stopped and woke Richard up. I told him that was the first time I had ever driven that far and that long. He never asked me to drive again.

Richard was released from the service and he went back to St. Louis, MO. His family owned a pizza restaurant. He promised free pizza if I ever came to St. Louis. Once when I was passing through St. Louis, I tried to find him but had no luck. I could not remember how he spelled his last name.

Johnny V. was from East St. Louis. He was a butcher by trade, but the Marine Corps saw him as a rifleman. After being together in the rifle company for a while, they realized he was better suited as a butcher than a rifleman. He was transferred to H&S Company and assigned to the mess hall. For Pete M., Richard O., and me, it was a great deal, because from that day forward, we had access to extra food! Every night after the movie, we all would go back to the mess hall and Johnny V. would feed us sandwiches, milk, and ice cream. It was great! When I left to go to Korea he was still working at the mess hall. I never saw him again.

Milton P. was from one of the New England states. I can't remember which one. He was a baseball player and had been signed to the New York Yankees farm team with a $500 signing bonus. He never reported because he was drafted first. Milton was a big country boy with a strong arm. He was always fooling around and never took the Marine Corps too seriously.

On board ship for a training exercise, Milton took the radio man's radio. This was a communication radio carried on your back—an expensive piece of equipment—and he threw it overboard! When it was discovered that it was missing, there was a complete search of the ship. They looked everywhere, but found no radio. Milton told me that they would never find it. I asked him how did he know; he said he just knew.

It didn't take the Marine Corps long to realize that Milton was a professional baseball player. He was transferred to play baseball for the Marine Corps team. Before he left, he admitted to me that he had thrown the radio overboard on that training exercise. I never saw him again. I never knew if he made it to the Major Leagues!

One day I was very depressed with the whole world and the Marine Corps in general, so I decided to go AWOL (Absent Without Leave). I asked Richard O. if he could draw up some phony leave papers for me, and he did. They looked really official. I went home and my dad asked to see my leave papers. They passed the test and I remained home for ten days.

When it was time to leave, I went down to Grand Central Station and turned myself in to the Military Police who were in that area. They took me to the Brooklyn Navy Yard and turned me over to the Marine detachment. I spent the night there, and in the morning, the sergeant major of the post gave me a ticket voucher for a train trip back to Camp Lejeune.

Upon arrival at Camp Lejeune, I was given a summary court martial. A summary court martial was a one-officer court. You told your story and the assigned officer sentenced you. I was sentenced to 30 days of hard labor without confinement. That meant that in the evenings, I had to go to the mess hall and clean the stoves, etc. It only lasted about three days, because the battalion had been preparing for deployment to Vieques Island, down in the Caribbean. Once deployment was underway, there was no more talk of continuing my hard labor sentence. I thought I got away with something at the time, but this would come back to bite me in the future.

The training in Camp Lejeune was endless. We went out in the field almost every day. Sometimes we rode but most of the time it was walk, walk, walk. Camp Lejeune is all flat land; there are no hills. When you're walking, you can see on and on forever, but forever never comes!

One day a friend of mine from the Bronx showed up looking for me. I was completely surprised— there, in Camp Lejeune, was my best friend, Billy T. I am not sure how he got there, but it was good to see him. I gave him some Marine Corps utilities so he would blend in and be able to get into the mess hall to eat. As our company was called out for chow, I told him to just stay by me and nobody would know. That night I found an empty bunk in the squad bay where he could sleep. At about 3:30 a.m., the duty NCO would go around and wake up all the people who had been assigned mess duty so they could get to the mess hall by 4:00 a.m. If you had been assigned mess duty, you placed your towel on the front of your bunk before you went to sleep. All others would place their towel on the rear of their bunk. Well, it seems that Billy T. didn't know that, and he placed his towel on the front of the bunk, and was now being harrassed to get up and get up now. I explained this to the duty NCO and we all went back to sleep,, but not for long as reveille was at 5:00 a.m.

That morning we were going out to the field and I had to say goodbye to Billy T. It was very cold that morning as we marched out of the area. I looked back at Billy T. and he was just laughing. The next time I saw him was after I returned from Korea and Japan. He had been in the Navy but was assigned duty in downtown New York. The Navy had an administration building there and he rode the subway to work. "Join the Navy and see the world," is what they say, but Billy T. didn't get to see any of it!

When stationed at Camp Lejeune, only one thing is certain, and that is that you are going to deploy to the island of Viequez. During this tour at Camp Lejeune, we made two trips to Viequez. The island is beautiful, and from the deck of an APA, it looks like it came right out of a Hollywood movie. The hills are lush green and the beaches sandy white.

The island is only about seven miles long and four miles wide. Three quarters of the island belongs to the US Navy. They have been using it for more than sixty years for naval gunfire and air strike,s and of course Marine Corps amphibious landings and helicopter assaults. Upon our ship's landing, we set up camp in a quickly-made tent city. We were to be ashore for about two weeks for intense training. It was during this trip to Vieques that I picked up a nickname.

It was supposed to be an easy exercise—a night compass march. We went out by squads, and starting at the base point, we would march off using our compass to find the first check point. At the first check point, we would receive a new compass reading to start off looking for the second check point, and so on, to the third and then the final leg home. At night it was difficult to pick out a landmark of some type to line up with your heading on the compass, so one would have a fellow Marine go forward as far ahead as he could, within sight range. Then one would line up on his compass reading, and move his partner left or right using signals, until he was in line with the compass reading. Then the Marine using the compass would move forward to meet his partner and repeat the procedure. On this particular exercise I was put in charge and off we went.

There were no NCOs with us, as they were all at the various check points. We hit the first check point right on the button, and in pretty good time. When we zoomed right ahead to the second check point, we really thought, *This is a snap.*

We were laughing and joking on the way to the third check point and again, right on to the last one. We were making record time and by the looks of it, we would finish the march in a little over four hours. Now we were on the way home. Boy, this seemed easy but the final check point (home base) wasn't coming into view. Time went by and still no checkpoint. We started to get worried now because we were long overdue and had no clue in what direction to go. The troops were now mumbling, cursing , moaning, groaning, and tired, and so was I. We walked for what seemed like forever. By then, it was 2:30 in the morning and we had no idea where we were. The exercise was supposed to be over at midnight.

I stopped the squad and said, "Let's stop right here," even though I didn't know where "here" was. We dropped our gear and settled down to get some sleep. I assured the squad that someone must be looking for us, and that if we stayed still, we would be found. Sleep came quickly!

At first light, I jumped up and saw that there was a dirt road about 100 yards from where we had stopped—it had not been visible in the dark. We packed up our gear and got on the road. We walked and walked, then saw a jeep coming at us. "Are you the guys who have been lost all night?" they asked. They called in to home base, saying that they had found us.

We were instructed to sit down not to move, that a truck was on its way. The truck took us back to the camp area. When we arrived, the company was in the morning formation, and as we rolled in, the whole company was laughing and clapping. Someone in the company yelled, "It's 'Back Azimuth' Landry!" ("Back Azimuth" is a method of finding your way: when you take a compass heading and you want to return to your original point, you simply add 180 degrees if your original heading was under 180 degrees, and you subtract 180 degrees if your original heading was over 180 degrees.)

It seems we stayed overnight in an impact area for live artillery fire. There was a fire exercise scheduled to begin at first light that had to be canceled because they didn't know where the hell we were. The company commander told me that even though we were lost, I did a good job of keeping everybody together and not letting them wonder all over the place. They called me "Back Azimuth" from that point on, but the name never followed to any other duty station.

It was during this two week training program that we went back onboard ships and made a before-dawn amphibious landing We were in a storm, and we all thought they would call the landing off because of waves. The swells were high. On making the landing, we were called from our quarters to our assigned debarkation stations. There are several stations around the ship, with Marines climbing down from all those stations. The first Marines down the net took hold of the net, pulling it away from the ship, thus making it easier for those who follow. The landing craft (Mike Boat) was bouncing all over the place, but Marines kept going down. I was the last to go down and on the way, a huge wave came, throwing all the Marines in the Mike Boat all over the place. The net holders dropped the net. That put me flat against the hull of the APA with the Mike Boat about to crash into the APA and me. I had no time to think, just to react.

I pushed myself backward, letting go of the net, and fell the rest of the way down to the landing craft. I landed on top of a bunch of Marines and luckily none of us were hurt. I was lucky to have caught the Mike

Boat as it was coming up rather than going down. If the Mike Boat had been going down, I could have easily fallen into the ocean, and with all the gear I was carrying and that heavy storm brewing, I would have been easily lost! Lady Luck was with me that day.

Back at Camp Lejeune, the talk was still about the Korean War. Everybody wanted to go. They used to announce every Friday, to sign up if you wanted to go to Korea. When they dismissed the formation, there was always a mad rush to the sign-up sheet. Those who were picked to go were delighted, and all others moaned and groaned that the war would be over before they could get there. A Marine is trained for war, and when there is one, he wants to be part of it. I even requested to speak to the battalion commander about going. He told me to be patient, my time would come.

KOREA
1952 - 1953

In late November my orders came: report to Camp Pendleton, California, for cold weather training before debarking for Korea. Just what I was waiting for. A quick trip home to the Bronx, a few farewell parties, and I was off to California. At Camp Pendleton we were fitted with cold weather clothes, issued rifles and 782 gear, and then trucked up to the Sierra Mountains in Northern California to a place called Pickle Meadows.

The problem facing us at Pickle Meadows wasn't the snow and ice, it wasn't our cold weather gear that we were lugging around, and it wasn't the mountainous terrain. It was the *heat*. It was *hot!* We were walking around in our undershirts. The instructors were telling us as we crossed a stream by walking a rope that we should make believe the rope was icy. As we pitched our tents for the night, we were told to make believe that we were in three feet of snow, and as we woke in the morning, to make believe the snow had completely buried our tents and we had to dig our way out. The weather was beautiful the entire week. We spent Thanksgiving eating c-rations. The training was fun and would have been a little more challenging if it were really in cold weather.

Then it was back to California and then on to San Diego to board a MSTS ship, destination Korea. At last I was underway to Korea. I had watched others go and looked forward to the day I would go. The trip took about 15 days. We stopped in Kobe, Japan, for one night. They didn't let us off the ship because we were to set sail in the wee hours of the morning.

Upon arrival in Korea, we were taken by train to a training area. It was a tent city. We spent a week there for introduction to Korea before being assigned to units. We had lectures all day every day, covering the climate, the people, the cold weather, the war, and so on.

It was a week or so before Christmas that we finally got assigned. We were again put on a train and headed north to our units. My unit was on the MLR (main line of resistance). When I checked in, I was told that my squad was out on an outpost and I would be joining them shortly. The next evening I joined a mule train—Korean Service Workers—out to the outpost. It was pitch dark as we set out. When we arrived at the outpost I was introduced to my squad leader and a few others who were around the CP.

My squad leader, a Sgt. S., told me to follow him, that he would place me on the line. As we walked along the trench line, we passed Marines in fighting holes. We stopped at one point and the Sgt. told the Marine there, "Here is your replacement. Fill him in."

The man I replaced told me, "The enemy is this way," pointing in front of where we were standing, "and the MLR is back there," pointing back to the area I had just come from, "and I'll be home for Christmas. 'Bye." I guess I was filled in! I spent the rest of that night staring into the darkness. After every noise I heard that night, I envisioned a 1000 enemy soldiers charging up the hill at me. Your mind plays funny tricks on you in the dark.

In the morning everyone went to sleep except one person who manned a prone position spot with a clear view of the Chinese hills. You will never guess who was assigned that spot that morning. You're right, it was the new kid—*me*. At first light, the trenches become empty really quick. I moved over to where I was to be the guard for the next four hours.

As I looked out toward the Chinese positions, I was shocked to see a Christmas tree, with presents and a big sign that said "Merry Christmas, Marines." I didn't know what to make of it, so I called the CP to ask the Lt. who had put the tree there. He came running and said a few curse words. It seems that the previous night, the Chinese placed the tree and sign right under our noses, in a part of the outpost that was manned by a machine gun team. They team caught hell for that.

The next night, we sent out four men to wire the tree, the presents, and the sign, and to bring the wires back to the trenches and then, all at once, pull them down. Nothing happened; the tree wasn't booby-trapped. The gifts were pulled into our trench and we opened everything. There were pens and paper, and of course, propaganda notices telling us this was Truman's War, not ours.

Life on the outpost was okay. We were awake most of the night and we slept during the day. We only moved around on the rear slope of the hill, as the forward slope faced the Chinese positions. We were out on the outpost for two to three weeks before being relieved.

One day the Lt. was going to the head, which of course was on the reverse slope. The head was just a hole and a wooden, one-man seat opening on top. My squad leader, Sgt. S., went to the forward slope and waved his hands wildly. It wasn't long before the whistle of mortars came pounding. The Lt. sitting on the throne grabbed his trousers, still down around his ankles, and came running into the trench. Sgt. S. came into our bunker laughing, "He didn't even wipe his ass!" Then it was off the outpost and back on the MLR. Life on the MLR is a little different from the outpost. On the MLR it was mostly patrolling. For my first couple of weeks out on the outpost nothing actually happened. I stood watch every night and that was about it. But back at the MLR, almost every night our platoon would be assigned a patrol. Sometimes the patrol was platoon-size, sometimes squad-size, sometimes fire-team size. One night our platoon was picked for a platoon-size patrol. On a platoon-size patrol, only two squads would go out, with the third held back as the angel squad. The angel squad was assembled and moved to a departure point, and if the actual patrol was hit, the angel patrol was immediately dispatched to its rescue. The angel squad carried out stretchers, if called, to bring back the wounded and the dead.

My first actual experience of war began when I was on an angel squad that was dispatched out because the patrol was ambushed. When a patrol is hit, they will call for mortars to box them in, meaning, "Drop mortars all around my position." When the angel squad is dispatched, the mortars are lifted so the angel squad can get to the patrol. On this particular night, I was with the angel squad when the word came about the patrol being ambushed.

When we arrived at the ambush site, there were a lot of casualties. Another Marine and I picked up a Marine that had his leg blown

27

halfway off. We put him on the stretcher and took off for the outpost. It was my first real glimpse of war and I never anticipated how I would react. They say that you shake after the action is over, not during it. And this is true.

We got about half way up the hill to the outpost when I stumbled and fell, dropping my end of the stretcher. The poor Marine went tumbling down the hill, getting his leg stuck in the barbed wire. We untangled him. He looked at us and said, "Let's try it again." When we got him on the outpost he said, "I guess I won't be playing baseball anymore," as calm as calm could be. It was a long night as we went back out to retrieve more casualties. Marines pride themselves of bringing the wounded back, if humanly possible. As long as there are wounded Marines out there, there will continue to be angle squads sent out to bring them back.

One of the guys in our platoon was 6'6" tall, and built like a flagpole. We were always kidding him about his height. He asked me one day what would happen if, when he was on patrol, he was wounded. How would we get him back? He was too tall for the stretcher. I told him that we would make two trips!

When he walked the trench line, his head was 6" above the trench. He had to stoop over. The poor guy worried about everything. When I returned after my trip to the hospital ship, he was gone. I never knew what happened to him. Back in the Bronx we had a guy just like him. We called him "Beans" and we used to kid him continually. He really was a nice guy, but very awkward. I don't know what happened to him either!

In really cold weather, we had to fire our rifles at first light if they had not been fired overnight. When we went out on patrols, we would place some kind of a target to shoot at in the morning. There was an old Korean graveyard in our patrol area, and when we would patrol that way, we would place grenades on the top of the headstones and try to shoot them off the next morning. The distance was too far away, but we kept trying.

One night on the MLR, we were on alert with 75 % watch. I was assigned to a fighting hole with another Marine. He was from New York. I can't remember his name. In any case, while we were in position, we talked about many things, and every once in awhile we just listened. Again, at night, when you hear a noise, you imagine the worst. The rule on the MLR was that if a Marine fired his weapon, he had better produce a body. They told us we had to go down to the wire to check if there was a body. Going out in no man's land, even down to your wire, was pretty scary.

All these rules, by the way, are told to you by the seasoned veterans who have been there at least a day longer than you. In any case, we were sure there was some movement out there. We were afraid to shoot so we decided to throw a grenade. We didn't want to take the blame for throwing a grenade at what could be nothing, so we threw the grenade in front of a machine gun bunker, so *they* would get the blame. And they did! Me and my buddy played dumb. Of course there was nothing out there.

The next morning, after firing our weapons, we settled down in our bunker to get some sleep. All of sudden, all hell broke loose. The stove pipe leading from our pot belly stove to the bunker roof was rattling like crazy as machine gun fire was blasting away on top of our bunker. The machine gunners were getting even for our grenade throw from the previous night. They had to fire their machine guns also, every morning, but they waited until we had finished and had settled down to get some sleep. Then they shot our stove pipe dead.

When we were on the MLR, there was hot chow, from 6 a.m. to 2 p.m. The only problem was that we had to walk three to four miles back to the rear to eat. There was also a designated time for showering and changing clothes. Before they put our rank on the collars of our jackets, we used to stencil our ranks on the sleeves ourselves.

When we took a shower, we turned in our dirty utilities and received a clean pair. They were not concerned about what rank was on the jacket, so we used to call it a shower promotion if someone got a jacket with a stenciled rank on the sleeve that was higher than his real rank.

When we went to eat, we always brought back a case of c-rations or a five gallon can of fuel for our stove. As for the c-rations, they were okay. We would open all the food and empty it out onto shelves we made so anybody could eat whatever they wanted when they wanted.

There was one c-ration item that nobody seemed to like. It was ham and lima beans. We had dug a big pit where we would throw away things we didn't want to eat. Somewhere in Korea there is a buried pit full of ham and lima beans.

There was a sign as you came near the MLR from the rear, that read, "DIG TO LIVE AND LIVE TO DIG." On a normal night on the MLR there was only 25% alert so we got plenty of sleep. However, the Marine Corps always want you moving and doing something, not just laying around all day. Hence the sign…The word would come around that they wanted everyone in the trench to dig and fill sandbags for a couple of hours.

When I first was on the MLR and the word came to dig, I kind of moaned and groaned but went out to dig anyway. A couple of the "old salts" said we wouldn't be out for long. They told me to sit down in the trench and they threw three hand grenades out over the trench. Boom! Boom! Boom! Off went the grenades and the phone rang. "What's going on down there?" the CP wanted to know. I bursted out laughing when I heard a Cpl. say, "It was mortars Lt . They see us digging."

"Secure digging." The word spread up and down the trench.

The Chinese had a propaganda loudspeaker that they would set up at various places and in the middle of the night they would sound off. If you are on watch when it comes on, it makes you think that they are talking to you! One night I was on watch and had just bent down to the bottom of the trench to light a cigarette under my poncho when the loud speaker came on, blaring, "Marines! It's okay to smoke…This is not your war…Go sit inside; it's too cold tonight!" Talk about feeling guilty. Then they would play music, and of course, more propaganda.

"Marines, where are your wives or girlfriends tonight? Who is with them? This is Truman's War, not yours!" They didn't stay in the same place for long, because as soon as we heard them, we would blast our artillery in their location. There would be a long period of silence, and then they would come on again, but from a different area.

Strange things happen when you are on the MLR. One night on watch, I was walking up and down the trench for no reason, when I saw a person jump into the trench from the forward slope. My heart stopped at first, then started pounding. I had been walking away from my position and I left my rifle there. I had to back step to get my rifle and then slowly move forward. I checked the chamber, making sure a round was in there, and I removed the safety. When I got to the spot where I saw someone jump in, there was no one there.

As I moved forward I saw another bunker. With my rifle, I moved the blanket away from the entrance, peeking in only to see two Marines sleeping and one sipping coffee. I think the Marine sipping coffee almost had a heart attack when he saw the rifle muzzle point at him from the dark. It seems that he had to take a leak, and he said it was easier to go right on the forward slope rather than going all the way back to the reverse side of the hill. I never walked away from my rifle again.

One night the squad I was attached to was assigned a patrol for that night. We were just sitting around (on our helmets) in our bunker, waiting for darkness to come. There were four of us living in the bunker. From outside someone pulled open the blanket that acted as a door, and asked if there was any out going mail. It was a friend of mine, George G. I called him and told him to come on in and have a cup of coffee. As he came in, I moved over, allowing him to put his helmet where I was sitting. When you are on the MLR you are pretty well spread out, so you get very little socializing done. When a friend comes by, you take the opportunity to chat. Just then, there was an explosion!

To this day, I don't know what exploded. The explosion knocked me on my back and the bunker filled with smoke. For a minute I could see nothing but a ray of light coming through where the blanket over the entrance was hanging. I tried to move towards the light but tripped over some bodies. About this time, Marines were there to assist us.

One of my boots was blown off and both my legs were bleeding. Of the five people in the bunker that night, I was the luckiest. One was hit in the neck, another in the groin area, with the third being hit in the stomach. My friend, who I invited in and who took the place where I had been sitting had half his face missing. On the way back to battalion aid, my friend lay on the stretcher next to me. He was breathing. I said a prayer for him and told him to hang on, but he couldn't. He was dead on arrival at battalion aid. The other Marines in the bunker were evacuated to Japan because their injuries were serious. I went to the hospital ship *Repose* for five days, and then was transferred to the hospital ship *Jutlandia* for the remainder of my days on the hospital ships. My injuries were anything but serious. Life aboard the hospital ship was not bad. We got three square meals a day and slept on clean sheets. If you had a broken bone anywhere, you automatically were sent to Japan. I had no broken bones!

Before I was transferred over to the *Jutlandia*, a member of my platoon came aboard. Pfc. S. was from Brooklyn, and boy, did he talk like it. He was being sent to Japan because he had been shot in the foot betwen two toes, breaking one of the bones. It seems he had been carrying a stretcher back into the outpost on a steep hill. He said he was pushing the stretcher while another was pulling it up, when a bullet hit him in the bottom of his foot.When the doctors, nurses or corpsman were not looking, he would jump up and down on his so-called broken bone and laugh, saying, "I'm going to Japan!"

When the *USS Repose* was ready to go to Japan I was transferred to the Danish hospital ship, *The Jutlandia*. There I remained 'til my legs were healed and I was ready to go back to my unit. This ship was different than the US hospital ship. The nurses were friendly, the doctors kept you abreast of your progress, and the crew was helpful. They even had a bar on the ship, but it was only open to officers.

One Marine asked me to take a picture of his wound. He had been shot in the ass, or I should say, *across* his ass. He bent over, and I took the picture with his camera. He had two long scars going from one cheek to the other.

On the night before I was to go back to duty, I was given brand new utilities, boots, etc. The next morning, another Marine and I decided to see if we could get into the bar on the ship. We asked a couple of nurses if we could borrow their rank insignias. Their insignias were the same as the Marine Corps' insignias. My buddy put on Captain bars and I put on 1st Lt. bars, and off we went to the bar. Unfortunately, it was closed. They only opened up in the evening. We gave back the insignias to the nurses, said our goodbyes, and headed ashore to go back to our units.

Once ashore, it took another couple of days to actually get to my unit. When I joined it, they were in reserve, completely off the MLR. Being on reserve is like being in heaven. There were movies every night and we received two beers a day. The shit had to hit the fan before you were called up. It was nice.

We had a song in Korea that was always a jinx. It was "Irene, Goodnight." Every time that song was sung or played on the radio, the next sound we heard was the rumble of trucks pouring into our area. Trucks coming into your area meant that the shit had hit the fan somewhere, and you were going back out there. One night during the movie, we heard the trucks coming and the film went dead. We were told to go back to our companies. We knew somebody was singing or humming "Irene, Goodnight" somewhere. We saddled up, got on the trucks, and off we went. We rode a long way and the artillery and mortar fire got louder and louder. Finally, we stopped and made our way up a hill on the reverse slope of the MLR. The line was being pounded and we were the back-up force. We were told to dig in. With mortar fire all over the hill, we dug quickly to get just below the surface, in the prone position.

Once I was in my hole, right below the surface, I covered myself with my poncho. Now, a poncho can barely protect you from the rain, but that night lying in a foxhole with my poncho covering me, I was as snug as a bug in a rug. I felt safe! We stayed there all night and in the morning the trucks returned to take us back to the reserve area.

There was a song someone had written about attacking a hill. I don't know if it's true; I was never involved. In any case, legend has it that it did happen, and the song is a tribute to a Lt. It was set to the tune of "On Top of Old Smoky."

It was three in the morning
the sun wasn't up
It was dark as the devil
as the troops saddled up
It was Able, Baker, and Charlie
assigned to the task

They knew not their mission
and they never did ask
But they looked at that hillside
with bunkers galore
And they knew that their mission
was hill 104
They jumped from the trench line
their heads they held high
They looked at their buddies
they knew some would die
Then they swept through the valley
with bayonnets fixed
And the Chinese held muster
with their 76.
The mortars fell heavy out of the sky
and that caused many brave men to die
The Chinese fought bravely
down to their last man
But soon on that hillside
the Marines overran
They looked all around for friends that they knew
And there on the skyline stood Jiggs Donahue
His arm it was bleeding, it was torn by a shell
The fighting was over, it was worse than all hell

Then somebody made up this tune up that we used to sing:

They promised us medals of silver
They promised us medals of gold
They made me a BAR man
I'll die when I'm 20 years old.

After our reserve period was over, it was back to the MLR and/or an outpost. My company went to the MLR. Army units had relieved the Marines and we were now taking back our original positions. We had been in reserve for about 3 weeks. We settled down to life on the MLR again. The first night back, the loudspeakers were blaring away. "Welcome back, Marines! We missed you! Now we have to get back to work!" And of course, there was their never-ending propaganda,

Some Army units stayed attached with the Marines on the MLR. All the Army guys carried automatic carbines. The only carbines the Marines had belonged to the officers and staff NCOs. But thanks to the US Army, many an enlisted Marine also. You see, when you went back to get a hot meal, all Marines carried their rifles with them at all times. The Army guys always laid their weapons outside the food line, only to find they had disappeared. In their places were usually rusty old M1 rifles.

Before we would go out on a patrol, we usually rehearsed the patrol on the reverse slope of the hill. Everyone would get in his respective positon. At the rehearsal, the only automatic weapons you would see were those of the platoon Sgt and the officers. You would also see each fire team with one man carrying a BAR. The BAR was a fully automatic weapon, but not very popular, because it was too heavy. It weighed almost 20 lbs. The carbine weighs 5 lbs. The Marine Corps standard issue rifle was the M1 and it was only semi-automatic weighing nine and a half pounds. At night when the patrol actually departs, a strange thing happens. Almost every man is carrying an automatic weapon. These are hidden by day and ready for patrol at night. Every once in awhile they would check in each bunker to see if there were any automatic weapons around. If they found one, the Marine would just say that he "found" it. It was not uncommon for a Marine to have a different weapon that he was issued. When in reserve, all the weapons are checked, and if your weapon is different, they just adjusted the record.

"Puff the Magic Dragon" was a sight to see. Puff was the two-engine DC3 plane with some kind of a gattlin gun. This gun fired incendiary rounds of 50 caliber ammunition that could cover a football field in seconds. Puff was used when under attack, to spray the enemy before they could advance to our position. At night, we couldn't see the plane but we could hear the engine, and all of a sudden, from out of the night darkness, came the roar of that gun. The incendiary rounds made a straight line from the plane to the ground. It was like the "Dragon" roared. It was awesome! I remember thinking, "Thank God *they* don't have one of them."

The last outpost I was on was called "toothache." It was partially in the zone neutralized by Panmunjom, the peace talks area. There was a sign on the outpost that read, "NO FIRING BEYOND THIS POINT." Can you believe that? We used to joke about it and jump on the no firing side of the sign and laugh and say, "They can't shoot me!" I don't know who the brilliant mind was that was behind the sign, but even the lowest Pvt. knows that you can't control the fragments of a mortar shell! Were we hit? No. Maybe we were just lucky.

Going out to outpost was always an adventure. We used a mule train. It was the KSC Korean Service Workers who carried out supplies to the outpost. There would be two Marines, one to lead and the other to bring up the rear. The workers used an "A" frame to carry their loads, and they went out *loaded*.

Sometimes a train was dispatched very early in the morning to get to the outpost before daylight. When they were coming out early in the morning, it was to work on the positions (bunkers and/or the trench line). A old story floating around was that one train checked out of the MLR with 20 men and arrived at the outpost with 21. When they called for instructions, they were told just to put them all to work!

On the way back in that night, they left the outpost with 21 and checked back into the MLR with 20. The extra man was an enemy infiltrator looking for a good meal, I suppose. The KSC workers could carry an unbelievable load on their "A" frames.

The cold weather training we received at Pickle Meadows California before coming over to Korea did not prepare us. There was nothing phony about Korea's cold weather. In the winter everyone looked overweight; we wore all the clothes we could put on, and then a parka on top. The mittens we used had one finger for pulling the trigger. They were pretty warm. The Mickey Mouse boots were a life saver. They were called Mickey Mouse boots because they looked like Mickey Mouse's feet! If we used just one pair of socks and moved our toes once in awhile, we were warm. The nights were extremely cold and the snow made it worse. I remember laying my rifle on the top of the trench with an extra bandolier of ammo and a half dozen grenades and covering them with empty sandbags to keep the snow off. It didn't take long before they completely disappeared—the snow was piling up that fast.

After the snow passed, Korea's rainy season was horrible. We stayed wet all the time. The trench would become muddy and sloppy. I remember one night coming in after a patrol to find that our bunker had caved in. Everything was floating around inside and not a dry spot in sight. I took a couple of ammo boxes and put them together to make a bed that would keep me out of the water. I threw down my air mattress, covered my self with my poncho, and slipped off into Dreamland. Somehow you survive!

You meet all kinds of guys in a war zone. Unfortunately, you can't remember them all. One platoon I was with had a whole squad of weird guys. They thought their squad was the best squad in the entire Marine Corps. They rarely ventured away from other members of the squad. They always wanted to be the point of any patrol they went on.

They called themselves the Raindrop Kids. They even made a sign and placed it in front of their bunker. They wrote the word "RAINDROP" vertically and made an acrostic out of it, writing a complementary word for each letter. For the life of me, I can't remember any of the words. We used to kid them all the time. We even had a song about them that really pissed them off. It went like this:

We are the Raindrop girls
We wear our hair in curls
We put our dungarees
Way up above our knees.

Like everyone else, they just faded away. In Korea you were here today and gone tomorrow. No explanations...it just happened.

I remember a guy we called Smiley. He had a smile on his face all the time. We have all seen people like him, I am sure, and here he was in the middle of Korea. One day while under a mortar attack, we were in the bunker waiting for the mortars to stop. There were three of us in the bunker at the time. The hill was taking a pretty good beathing and we waited patiently for the barrage to stop. As soon as that happened we had to man the trench, in case of an assault on the hill. Sitting on the dirt floor of the bunker, Smiley picked up an entrenching tool and started scratching at the dirt floor with the tool, saying, "We better dig in." Pfc T. got real upset and started yelling at Smiley to stop kidding around, but Smiley went right on scratching the floor, with a smile on his face. "Who's kidding?"he asked. All three of us were scared, but Smiley was just trying to break the tension we all felt. As soon as the barrage lifted we rushed out to man our positions.

When I looked around, Pfc T. was not there. I was the fire team leader and this was my fire team. I went back in the bunker and found Pfc T. still sitting on the floor. I told him to get outside to his position. He didn't move. I then told him that I would shoot him if he refused to man the line. He got up mumbling something under his breath, but he went outside. Would I have shot him? I really don't know. All I knew was that everybody was scared but we had a job to do and by God if I was out there putting my life on the line, he would be too. A week or two later he was transferred out of the unit.

The rumor spread like a wild fire: they signed a peace treaty, the war is coming to an end., we're going home. We all waited for the official word but it didn't come. We thought it was another false alarm. But then one day the word did come. Yes, the war would be over on July 27, 1953, at 10 p.m. My mind raced back to another July 27th that I was familiar with. It was July 27, 1950 that I enlisted in the Marine Corps.

On the evening of July 27th, I was called to the CP by my Platoon Sergeant. He told me that at 10 p.m. tonight, all firing would cease. All up and down the line, white star clusters would be shot, signaling the cease fire. However, up until 10 p.m., we were still at war. He wanted me to take my fire team out on a listening post. He told me we were NOT to engage the enemy, only listen and report. If we heard anything, we were to report and then move back. Not particularly thrilled with the assignment (after all this was the last few hours of the war), I went back and informed my fire team of our mission. Needless to say, none of them were thrilled either.

As soon as it turned dark we were off, out through the wire about 1000 yards in front of the MLR. We were just far enough away to be able to get a message sent if someone was coming, and then make it back. We settled down and listened. The hours went by slowly. All was quiet. We felt very lonely as we waited for the clock to strike 10. I looked at my Marine Corps issue watch and it said 9:30. Thirty minutes to go and it would be over. Just then all hell broke loose.

From both sides, artillery fire rained on enemy hills. We sat in the middle. What was going on? Did this mean the war was not going to be over at 10 o'clock? We kept looking from one side to the other. The CP told me to hold our position. But then at 10 o'clock it happened. The firing stopped and the night was lit up with white star clusters all up and down the line, from both sides. We all stood up just looking around. We saw people from both sides lighting up cigarettes right out in the open. Yes it was true, the war had ended. That night, we sat on top of the trenches instead of in them. We smoked, laughed, and speculated on what was going to happen .

Someone said the Marine Corps will probably make us police up the hill. We all nodded in agreement. And policing is what we did. The word filtered down. The next day we had to dismantle the bunkers, empty out all the sandbags and pile them in stacks of 50. Then we had to salvage all the lumber that was used on the bunkers.

We were told we had 3 days, and then we would have to be off the hill and move X number of meters back. That had been established in the peace agreement. The Chinese, of course, were doing the same thing.

We worked around the clock to make the deadline. We caved in the trenches and then we were trucked back to where the new line would be established. New camps were set up to house all the Marines coming off the line. Once they were established, it was back to the good old Marine Corps way. We used to call it Camp Lejeune, Far East. Some said the war was easier.

The tour in Korea was 13 months. When the war ended, I still had 5 months to go. I had joined the Corps in July 1950 for 4 years and my enlistment was up July 1954. So I had a year to go, with 5 months of the year in Korea. All people with under a year left to serve were interviewed for possible re-enlistment. Once I left Korea, I would only have seven months left in the Corps.

During the interview I made them an offer. I would re-enlist if, instead of sending me back to Camp Lejeune, they sent me to Japan for my remaining seven months! They agreed to send me to Japan, under the stipulation that I had to re-enlist immediately. Re-enlisting now was not what I wanted to do. In fact, I didn't want to re-enlist at all. I just thought that if I went to Japan for seven months and my enlistment expired while I was there, I would refuse to re-enlist and they would have to send me home. They turned me down.

Time went by and I was sent to temporary billeting, awaiting orders from Marine Corps Headquarters. I was going home. But at the eleventh hour, I was called back to the recruiter and told that they would send me to Japan, that I could re-enlist over there. I was happy as a lark. Camp Lejeune was the pits. By the way, I had been promoted to Corporal. Good duty....seven months in Japan, then home and out. Life was good.

YOKOSUKA, JAPAN
1953 - 1956

Yokosuka was a Japanese naval base taken over by the US Navy after the war. It was in the evening when I arrived, and I had just been given a place to sleep for the night. During the night, some of the Marines were coming back to the barracks after liberty, making lots of noise. In the morning, they wanted to know why I wasn't with them the previous night. Most of the Marines in the barracks had been in Korea for over 13 months; was time to let their hair down.

I spent the next couple of days getting issued all new uniforms, including dress blues. They didn't issue the dress blues in boot camp. There was no need for them. I was assigned to the brig. I had never worked in a brig before, but it looked like easy duty. Besides, I only had seven months to do in the Corps. At the brig I was assigned as the "turnkey." Turnkeys were on duty in the brig four hours on and eight hours off, for a 24-hour period. During the 24-hour period you were on, you did not get liberty. During the next 24 hours, you were not assigned to the turnkey desk. You got liberty at regular liberty hours, but during the working day, we did typical Marine Corps things.

Inside the brig, there was a desk about four to five feet above the deck looking down at the prisoners that were inside the cage. From the desk, you could see the entire inside of the brig, so you observed all the prisoners. Most of the prisoners in the brig were sailors serving under 30 days of confinement. Usually over-30-day prisoners were sent to the Tokyo stockade. But sometimes a tria lwas held up for whatever the reason, and the prisoner remained in the brig, even up to a year.

When I was working at the brig, I received another nickname. This time it was "Little Caesar." When I was on duty as the turnkey I followed the brig rules and regulations almost to the letter. For example, on Sundays, the prisoners who went to church went with shotgun-carrying Marine guards and sat in the back row all by themselves and the guards. Most of the prisoners found this too humiliating so they didn't go.

When I was on duty on a Sunday, I would gather all the prisoners in a circle with their military issue Bibles, have them sit down, then call on a prisoner to stand and read aloud. He would read until I called another prisoner to continue. I used to tell them that the Marine Corps says that you should have Religion on Sunday, and if you don't go to church then we will conduct our own services here. All the time they were reading aloud, I was sitting up at the turnkey's desk with my feet up, reading a dirty book. The prisoners hated this.

The prisoners were not allowed to smoke more than four cigarettes a day—one after every meal and one before lights out. We kept the prisoners' shaving gear and cigarettes under lock and key outside the cage. Inside the cage, there were two parallel white lines painted right in front of the turnkey's desk.

That was were all the prisoners stood whenever the turnkey said, "All prisoners on the white line!" They would drop whatever they were doing and run to the white line. Prisoners were not allowed to speak directly to a turnkey or a guard. If they wished to speak, they would stand on the white line and say, "Turnkey, sir, Prisoner [his name] requests permission to speak to the turnkey, sir."

After a meal, I would get the prisoners on the white line for their cigarettes. I passed out all the cigarettes, making sure that the prisoners would only get their own cigarettes. After all the prisoners had a cigarette, I would then light only the first cigarette and have the light passed down 'til all were smoking. I didn't give them a whole lot of time for the smoke, and many times I picked up the cigarettes before they were finished. It all depended on how I felt that day. Of course, all butts were collected and accounted for.

It was the night cigarette that I liked to pass out. We gave them a cigarette at a certain time with only a certain amount of time remaining until lights out. They had to get their cigarette in that window of time. I would open the cabinet, take out the cigarettes and put them in a box and place the box on the front of my desk, clearly visible to the prisoners. I would then call out, "All prisoners on the white line!" As soon as the prisoners were assembled on the white line at attention, I put my feet up on the desk and picked up my book to read. The sound of silence…you could hear a pin drop. And then one of the prisoners would speak up. "Turnkey, sir, Prisoner [his name] requests permission to speak to the turnkey, sir." I told him to speak. "Turnkey, sir, I think I hear a song coming on, sir."

Then I would ask, "What's the name of the song you wish to sing?"

With a very low, mumbled voice, he answered, "'The Marine Corps Hymn.'"

"I CAN'T HEAR YOU!" I yelled.

He would speak a little louder and I would keep yelling, "I CAN'T HEAR YOU!" Finally, they would realize they were running out of time because there would be no cigarettes if the bell for lights out were sounded. They all joined in, shouting louder now, "THE 'MARINE CORPS HYMN,' SIR!" They mumbled the singing at first, but after I yelled, "I CAN'T HEAR YOU!" enough times, they saw things my way and belted out a loud "Marine Corps Hymn." They sang so loud we had complaints from the officer of housing, whose office was nearby. The prisoners hated this most of all!

The prisoners didn't like to see me coming to work on house cleaning day. To me, house cleaning time was any time I was on duty during daylight. I would have the prisoners empty the cage, taking all racks and bedding outside in the yard to air out, then I would have the prisoners on their hands and knees with scrub brushes, scrubbing the cement floor of the brig. I would have them all scrubbing for the entire four hours I was on duty.

Our yard was not very big, so when we had the prisoners out in the yard for some close order drill they had to half step. While drilling, I would give them the "Escape Prisoner" command. As soon as they heard that command, all prisoners had to drop to the deck while the guard loaded the shot gun. The last prisoner standing when the guard yelled, "Escape Prisoner," was designated as the one escaping, and he was the one who got shot. When you are in a small, confined area, completely fenced in, and you give the "Escape Prisoner" command near the fence, getting down on the ground is difficult.

One time, a fellow Marine from the Marine barracks was a prisoner placed in our brig. During daylight hours, we yelled and harassed him, showing absolutely no favoritism. But after lights went out and all were asleep we would slip the Marine prisoner out of the cage and take him out in town for a good time, making sure he drank sparingly. After a few hours in town, we would slip him back in the cage. The next morning, we would start yelling and harassing him again. He was only with us for a week or so, and then he moved to the Tokyo stockade. He never returned to duty.

At about this time, my enlistment was coming to an end. The recruiter called me to his office and talked to me about re-enlisting. I did not even hesitate. I signed up for four more years.

We had two prisoners who were in the brig for almost a year. There were serious charges against them. One had killed another sailor in a bar room fight, and the other stole a semi truck loaded with American cigarettes. He sold the entire truckload of cigarettes and sent all the money home. He was on his way home when he was pulled off the plane at the last minute. These two prisoners were assigned to the supply room and the laundry detail in the brig. They were two tough, mean individuals, and if there was ever any problem with any prisoner, you could always count on these two to take care of it.

One night I was on the midnight to 4 a.m. turnkey shift, when an individual was brought into the brig. He was drunk as a skunk, loud, and obnoxious. As soon as he was in the brig, I was getting ready to assign him a rack to sleep it off. The "lifers" (so to speak) came up to the cage and said that they would put him to bed. I put the prisoner inside the cage and the night became quiet. Because they helped us out, we always excused them from any drilling or cleaning. We never had to lay a hand on a prisoner, because of the privileged two.

The prisoners' food was cooked at the base mess hall, then trucked to the brig. We had a topside room on the annex building in the compound where the prisoners ate. There was a refrigerator and a stove available there. The privileged two would always serve the food. One day they mentioned to me that the mess hall sent out a pound of butter for every meal and that it just got wasted. They told me that butter brings a premium price on the black market and they knew where to go to dump it.

From that day on, the prisoners got only a slab of butter, the privileged two were stashing the butter away in the refrigerator. One pound of butter was lasting three or four days. The butter was sold on the black market. We had drinking money for a couple of months.

When a prisoner did something wrong we would place him on report. Whatever little privileges he had would be taken away from him for a period of time. If he continued to cause problems, he would receive a week or ten days of diminished rations. Diminished rations meant that he would only get a little of everything to eat, not a full meal. People on diminished rations were also housed in a private cell, away from all other prisoners. Their food would be brought to their cage on a tray and the prisoners would sit and eat under the eye of the turnkey. If the tray contained more than a spoonful of each item, the turnkey would remove the excess and throw it away before the prisoner sat down to eat.

A new commanding officer had taken over command of Marine barracks. He was Colonel Leonard F. Chapman. It really was the changing of the guard. The colonel was indeed different. The duty at Marine barracks was great "BC" (or "before Chapman," as we said), but he brought change. The Marine barracks was a "semi-" spit-and-polish detachment BC, but quickly became high gloss when he took over.

We were all fitted for white trousers to with go our dress blues in summer. White trousers were not part of the original issue. Inspections became a regular thing, as did the Friday Parade on the parade ground in front of Marine barracks. He had a barber placed in Marine barracks, claiming that Marines needed a haircut every week, and they didn't have time to wait in the Exchange barber shop.

There was a daily morning inspection, followed by close order drill. And of course, there was exercise every morning at reveille. There was no doubt that this man was going some place in the Corps. And we were right. He went up the ladder to become the commandant of the Marine Corps, the only four-star general the Marine Corps had at that time.

Back at the brig, he placed a complaint box in the cage with only the ODat Marine barracks authorized to open the box and deliver the complaints to him. The box had to be emptied every day. One night while checking out for liberty, I was in the duty warden's office waiting for the duty warden to come to the desk, when the phone from the turnkey's desk inside the brig rang. I picked it up and the turnkey said he had a couple of prisoners acting up and he wanted to know what to do. I just told him to make them "duck walk" 'til they dropped and that should do it. Then I went out on liberty.

The next day, a captain from Marine barracks came to the brig, advising the brig officer that the brig was under investigation for mistreatment of the prisoners. A letter from the complaint box claimed that we, the guards, were subjecting the prisoners to cruel and unusual punishment.

The captain spent about two weeks interviewing everyone, prisoners and guards. His conclusion was that he could not pinpoint anyone in particular for mistreatment, but the turnkey on duty the night of the duck walk incident looked suspicious, and that I was also involved.

The duty turnkey and I both were called to the colonel's office. The turnkey involved was a sergeant, and when he came out of the colonel's office, he told me that he lost a stripe. I was next. I stood at attention as the colonel said that there was no evidence against me. "Do you have anything to say?" he asked. My response was, "I have nothing to say." I was dismissed and that was the end of that investigation.

I was, however, transferred from the brig back to Marine barracks into the military police unit. There was an indoctrination period that I had to go through, and before long, I was assigned to patrol unit. We rode in a MP jeep, with me riding shotgun. I didn't have a military driver's license. On that first patrol, we were scheduled for the 4-8 shift. We went on at 4 p.m. and off at 8 p.m, then back on patrol from 4 a.m. until 8 a.m. It was uneventful. The action shift was 8 p.m. 'til midnight, and the most boring shift was 4 a.m. to 8 a.m.

Getting my military driver's license was difficult for me. My driving experience was extremely limited. To get the license, you had to take a driving test. The test consisted of driving a jeep through an outlined course, straight ahead, with a 90-degree left turn, then a 90-degree right turn, then straight ahead again. That was no problem. The problem was what came next: having to drive the course in reverse without hitting any of the cones that marked the course. I failed! I knocked down all the cones and was told to practice and then come back. I went back and again failed and failed and failed.

Then one day, the Japanese employee who was in charge of the driving course was placing the cones along the painted course when a huge storm hit, and it poured down rain. He was racing around, trying to pick up all the cones and I helped him. When we had them all picked up and inside the shed, he thanked me for my help. He knew me quite well by this time because I had been trying the course over and over again. We waited to see if the rain would let up but it didn't. As I started to leave, he told me to wait a minute and asked for my ID card. He then proceeded, without a word, to type. In a minute or so he handed me my military driver's license and said, "Congratulations, you passed."

Now with a new military driver's license in my hand, I pitched my case for a patrol. It fell on deaf ears as the platoon sergeant told me I had to get in line and wait, that everyone wanted to drive. We had been using Jeeps for patrol vehicles, but in early 1954, we received a fleet of brand new Chevy "black-and-whites." With new vehicles came a whole bunch of dos and don'ts—mostly don'ts. The vehicles were inspected at the changing of the guard at 8 a.m. every morning. The guards went over them with a fine tooth comb. When we were using the Jeeps, no one seemed to care what happened to them, after all, a Jeep is a Jeep. But brand new 1954 Chevy "black-and-whites?" They cared.

My time finally came and I was assigned to drive one of those new patrol cars at the Marine sub station in Zama, about 25 miles outside of Yokosuka. It was mostly highway patrol work. Many Americans lived in the Zama area, and we patrolled the highways around the clock. It was very boring work—all the action was going on in Yokosuka.

All we did was drive around and around and around for four hours. We perked up when we would run low on gas because then we had to go to Yokosuka to fill up on base. Once the desk sergeant. gave us permission, we were off to Yokosuka and hoping that we would get a radio call to assist the Yokosuka patrols. We would call in to the Yokosuka station telling them we are in to fill up, but available if needed.

We never got called, so we decided to make our own excuse for action. There were three sailors staggering down the street and we pulled over to stop them. Getting out of the car, we asked to see their ID cards and liberty passes. The staggering was more exaggerated than real. A lot of the sailors have a few beers and act drunk, but it's mostly a show for the girls. We told them to head back to their ship.

One day on the four to eight shift, I was assigned a new shotgun rider. He was a new guy and this was his first patrol. This was the longest four hours I have ever spent. This guy *never* opened his mouth for the entire shift—not a single word! I talked and tried to get him to say something, but had no luck. He just sat staring straight ahead. As we were heading back to the station to be relieved after our shift, he asked, "Do you like blue socks?" Can you believe that? I screamed, "What the f*ck are you talking about?" He just smirked and said nothing. He was nicknamed "No Talk."

We did have fun at the sub station though. Sometimes when we went into Yokosuka to fill up the gas tank, we would pick up a girl and take her out to the Zama area. We would drive out to the beach and have some fun and then sneak her back into town.

One night when we were trying to get a girl back into Yokosuka, we saw the red flashing lights of a Japanese police road block ahead. The Japanese police often set up road blocks to stop people from coming in to Japan illegally. We didn't want to get caught with the girl in the car, so I told her to hold on, turned on my red light, and hit the siren. Once the police saw and heard us coming, they removed the road block and we plowed past them, not even slowing down.

We were told not to stop any car with blue license plates. Blue license plates belonged to embassy employees, those of our country and every other country. One day at a meeting, prior to going on duty, we were again reminded not to stop any car with blue license plates; it seemed someone had stopped a Russian embassy car for speeding. The patrol officer didn't give the driver a ticket but just stopping the car was enough to cause an uproar.

The patrol driver on shift at that particular time swore up and down that it wasn't him who stopped the car. The Russians failed to get the patrol car number, so there was no way they could pin it on anyone. The very next night, the Russian embassy car was stopped again and given another lecture, then let go. At the morning meeting, the subject came up again and the patrol driver from the night before denied being the one responsible for the incident. We all sat there thinking that maybe it was one of those smart asses from Yokosuka fooling around in our area, putting the blame on us.

Then the OD showed us all a blown-up 12 x 12 inch picture of the patrol driver in question, leaning out the open window of the car, waving his finger in the Russian's face. We all broke up laughing. The driver was relieved of duty and sent back to Marine barracks in Yokosuka. He was never again allowed to patrol outside of the base. We used to kid him, telling him that we saw two strange guys with long black overcoats standing right across from the main gate. We told him they looked like they were angry Russians and were probably waiting for him to come outside the gate.

When you came off duty, we always cleared our pistols before turning them in. To clear the pistol, we would remove the magazine, pull the slide to the rear, look in the chamber to make sure no round was in it, release the slide, then fire the empty pistol into a sand barrel by the desk sergeant's desk. On this particular night, a Sgt. G. coming off duty cleared his pistol, but instead of firing it into the barrel, he pulled the trigger without thinking and BANG went the gun. The bullet hit the desk, sergeant, paralyzing him for life. Sgt G. was relieved from duty and I really don't know what happened to him. He was just gone. He was shipped back to the States and I guess he was court martialed.

Duty at the sub station in Zama was very laid back. We all wanted to get sent back to Yokosuka where all the action was. The only sailors we saw at Zama were the married ones, and they rarely got into any trouble. Once in awhile there was a little domestic problem but all in all, it was very quiet. After a period of time I was sent back to Yokosuka.

The patrol cars in Yokosuka were manned by a Marine driver and a member of the Seaman Guard. The Seaman Guard were sailors but they lived in Marine barracks and did what we did. They used to refer to themselves as "junior jarheads." At the sub station in Zama, the patrol cars were manned by two Marines. The Seaman Guard were very good and you could trust them. You didn't feel so alone entering a bar with one of them with you. They didn't stay too long in the Marine barracks and I think that Col. Chapman probably got rid of them. When that happened we picked up naval personnel from the ships in port that day to ride with us.

From the beginning, riding with the SP from the ships in port was a problem. This was our job, our *only* job; we were trained and practiced it daily. To them, it was just a lousy assignment for one night. It got so bad that we would not enter a bar unless another Marine patrol car backed us up. The new instructions given to the Navy SPs let them know exactly what their job was; it wasn't just to pick up the Marine's helmet if it fell off. If a Marine got into a tussle, then those SPs had better be in that tussel too. If a Marine got his uniform torn up, the SP's uniform had better be torn also. In other words, their superior officers were saying, "Do your job." Col. Chapman also let it be known that if a Navy SP failed to do his job, charges would be filed against him. We never trusted the SPs much, and always relied on another Marine.

Before the Seaman Guard had been re-assigned somewhere, I had one of them as my shotgun rider. I remember entering a bar right across the street from the main gate. The entrance to the bar had a curtain hanging down so that you had to push or pull the curtain away to enter. My partner and I had parked our car nearby and decided to enter this particular bar.

As I pushed the curtain aside, a fist came flying through the air, hitting me smack in the nose. Down I went, with blood streaming all over the place. After I stood up and cleared my head, both my partner and I charged into the bar, swinging our clubs. There were four sailors in there. We knocked them all over the bar and had them pinned on the floor. We only had two sets of handcuffs so we cuffed them together in pairs. We called for the paddy wagon to pick them up. I had to return to the base to change my shirt and get back on patrol.

Each night before we went on duty, we were instructed by the OD what to watch for. On this night, we were told to make sure all the sailors had their sleeves rolled all the way down. A lot of sailors would roll their cuffs up to show off the dragon design sewn into the back of the cuff, but it was strictly illegal.

The bar was crowded, as most bars usually were when a fleet was in. As we walked around the bar, we got the usual sarcastic cat calls, but from the distance, never to our faces. After the sailors had a few beers in them, having girls all around them made the sailors into tough guys. As I stopped at one table, I asked a sailor to please roll down his sleeve. The girls at the table heckled us, along with the other sailors at the table. Soon other tables were joining in. The unwritten rule was, when in a bar and having trouble with a person, remove that person from the bar. This usually keeps other sailors and girls from instigating more trouble. I again asked the sailor to roll his sleeves down. All I got was, "F*ck you!" I reached down to pull him from the booth. As I pulled him up from his sitting position, he began to straighten up, and up and up and up he went. He was about 6'5". My mind was racing. *How am I going to get this big SOB outside?* I wondered. I remembered a lecture about how to bring big people down.

"Go for the shins!" they always advised. With my club, I hit this giant across his shins and over and down he went. My partner and I then dragged him out of the bar, and before he knew what had happened to him, he was cuffed and lying face down on the street. We called the paddy wagon.

There was an area in Yokosuka that was called the Joyful Kingdom. It was the worst part of town and most people avoided it. My partner and I were assigned to patrol this section so we stopped the car and walked around. There was one thing that was never allowed anywhere, and that was drinking on the street. On this particular night there were about eight sailors standing out side of a bar, drinking. Seeing us didn't phase them at all. As we approached them and asked them to go back inside to drink, they started in on us. "What the f*ck are you doing in our area? You f*cking Marine ^%$&%, kiss my a**!" By this time they had walked completely around us. We were in the center and I looked at our car about 100 feet away. At the time, 100 feet seemed like a mile.

I told the sailors it was okay, that there was, no problem. We started moving slowly toward the car. They continued laughing and cursing at us. We continued moving towards the car. After we got into the car, we locked the doors and got on the radioed for help. The station call sign was "Bluff Peter," and we were "Bluff Peter 2." I relayed, "Bluff Peter, this is Bluff Peter 2. Allstar. Allstar at Joyful Kingdom."

An "Allstar" call summoned all cars to the scene, even all off-duty Marines at the station. We listened to the cars responding to the "Allstar" command and now could hear sirens heading this way. It didn't take long. As the patrol cars came roaring into the Joyful Kingdom we got out of our car and, with smiles on our faces, lit into the mob. We filled up three paddy wagons and cleared out all the bars in the Joyful Kingdom.

Yokosuka was a wide open town. When the fleet was in, you could see nothing but white hats on the street. Many ships would have parties ashore at various hotels, etc. All parties had to be registered with the military police. Many times these parties had to be broken up before they tore down the building.

When called to an "Allstar" at a party, all military police would meet outside and then after we all were assembled, we would march right down the middle of the party room, splitting the group in half. Then we would take the troublemakers outside by groups and put them on busses to take them back to their ship. When the fleet was in, military police were working overtime every night. When the fleet was out it was kind of routine with just enough drunks to keep the patrols busy.

One of the biggest complaints against the Marine military police was that we were using to much force when trying to get a sailor out of a bar and back to his ship. At least that was the story the sailors told their captain to get off the hook for being drunk and disorderly—it was the Marines' fault!

One night, the commanding officer of a ship in port wanted to ride around with a Marine patrol to see how things were handled. I was stuck with him and I was told to take him wherever there was a disturbance, so he could see for himself how his people acted. I responded to every call that night, along with the assigned patrol. As I recall, it was one hell of a night.

The captain observed everything that night. He got an eyeful and an ear ful. He watched as paddy wagon after paddy wagon was called out to take the sailors down to the station. At the station, he saw and heard how his people acted when asked a question or given a command. And when the night was over, his comment to the OD was that he was surprised at how polite the Marines were, when first approaching a sailor, and that it was usually the sailor who provoked the Marine into taking action. He also sent a letter to Col. Chapman, complimenting the Marines. I pity the poor sailor in that captain's his command if the sailor was ever sent back from liberty.

There was one bar in Yokosuka that we all visited on *and* off duty. When on duty, we would go in the back and get a drink and something to eat, all on the house. The *mama san* owning the place wanted to make sure that if there was trouble in her bar, we would respond fast. There were some other places in town where we couldn't get any freebies. Ironically, when those places called for our help, we would have an usually hard time finding where those places were. We gave them a little time to sit and watch the sailors tearing up their bar, with no military police showing up until it was all over and the guilty sailors were long gone. The stingy owners usually came around and learned to be a little more accommodating.

Another thing we would do to uncooperative bar owners was to check their bar every hour. A military police patrol would enter the bar and announce, "All military people outside." Once outside, we would stand in the doorway and ask each sailor to show his ID card and liberty pass. We would check their IDs and then tell them they could go back in. With us standing in the doorway, no sailor would go back in; they would just go to a different bar. An hour or so later, another Marine patrol could would appear at the same bar and do the same thing. It drove the *mama sans* crazy, but they got the message—cooperate, or else...

On a routine check of the Joyful Kingdom, a Marine MP and his Navy partner went into a bar. The Marine had gone upstairs just to look around, and as he started coming down, he was hit in the back of the head with a bottle, causing a sever concussion. The Marine was hospitalized and sent back to the States. Our commanding officer, Colonel Chapman, was furious and called for a meeting of all MPs.

At that meeting he told us we were not going to let that assault go unpunished. He called for "Allstars" nightly to clear out all bars and upstair rooms in the Joyful Kingdom. Every evening, we were told when the "Allstar" would occur, and at that time we converged on the Joyful Kingdom. We did it nightly for the first week, and after that, a couple of times a week. After the second week, the Joyful Kingdom was deserted. Most of the sailors found others places to go.

We all knew that we were not to take our cars out to the Japanese gas stations for any reason. All our cars were serviced and cleaned on the base. It was the morning of New Year's Day, and the word came that there was going to be a vehicle inspection and that cars had to be cleaned. I was coming off the four to eight shift and there was no way I could get to the base and get my car cleaned in time for inspection, because the line was long. I thought, *The hell with it. I will go to a Japanese gas station and for 100 yen (a quarter), get it cleaned fast.*

So there I was standing in the open, in my uniform, with all the Military Police accessories on, just waiting for the attendant to finish my car. I looked up in time to see Col. Chapman staring at me as he drove by in his own car. I told the Japanese boy, "*Hiyaku! Hiyaku!*" (which meant, "Hurry! Hurry!"). At about that time, into the gas station drive way comes the colonel's car. I thought, *I'm dead!* As the colonel exited his car, I greeted him with a great big salute and "Good morning, Sir."

He said, "Good morning, Corporal Landry," and asked if we had been busy the night before (New Year's Eve). I told him very busy. Then he asked if I had the Christmas holidays off. I told him I did and he said, "Carry on." I saluted and he left. I had to work one of the holidays but I got the other one off. I dodged another bullet!

When the commandant of the Marine Corps came to visit us, the whole barracks was in an uproar. Everything had to be just right, because if we failed the commandant's inspection, only God knew what Col. Chapman would do. Anyway, we were prepared for an inspection outside on the parade grounds. That morning, however, the rain came and it poured. We laughed and said, "There goes our outside inspection. If they want to inspect, they will have to inspect us standing by our bunks." That's what we thought; Col. Chapman had another idea.

We were in our dress blues, so the colonel had a bus take us back to the barracks as many Marines as possible, standing up, so that our uniforms would not get any wrinkles. We also had to walk on our heals of the shoes so we didn't put a crease in the shoe. The bus took us to the Navy gym and after all of us were assembled, the commandant came, made his walk through, and was gone. Going back to the barracks on the bus, we could sit down and walk normal.

The colonel's time with us was up and he was assigned to Washington, D.C. It was the beginning of his climb to the prestigious position of commandant. Before he left us, we all assembled in the base movie theater and he made his farewell speech. One of the last things he said was that if any of us had a problem or needed something, to drop him a line and he would see what he could do.

His replacement showed up about a week later. This one was another colonel and I don't remember his name. He didn't stay long because he died in his sleep the first weekend he was here. Another parade was scheduled, this time for a military funeral with all the bells and whistles. As we slow-marched in the procession, we were all wondering, *Who will be next?* The next commandant showed up a week later with his dog!

During this tour in Japan, my best friends were Robert S., from Erie, Pennslyvania, and John H, from Detroit, Michigan. We were the original three amigos. Robert S. was a big guy who drank like a fish. He could easily consume a fifth of anything, all by himself, at one sitting. He lost all his teeth at a young age and he was always going to the dentist, getting fitted for new teeth. He used to ride the base bus for hours and hours while he was supposed to be visiting the dentist, and later tell the platoon sergeant when he returned that he had to wait at the dentist's office. He did this continually. When he got his first set of teeth, he deliberately stepped on them and then claimed that while out in town, someone sucker-punched him and his teeth fell out, and during the fight someone stepped on his teeth.

John H was a smaller guy, but tough. He really was a squared-away Marine and always looked good in his uniform. He also was a heavy drinker, but not up to Robert S. level. He would never go out at night before everything was prepared for the next day. He would never loan anyone anything. Years later, while serving together in Hawaii, he changed his tune. But more about that later.

The schedule read, "Grab Ass Day!" It meant that after lunch, everyone was prohibited from going back into the barracks and had to participate in some sort of sports activity. Just lying around was not permitted. It was a beautiful day and me and my amigos headed for the boat dock, where we checked out a rowboat.

Off we went with one rowing and the other two giving instructions. Destination: "Monkey Island." We thought it would be a snap to row over to the island, but as time went by and the island still remained far in the distance, we began to wonder. We all took turns rowing, with the other two voicing their opinions on how best to paddle and steer.

The Yokosuka shore was now far behind us, and Monkey Island was still way off in the distance. All of a sudden the weather turned. The sky darkened and ripples in the water became more frequent. We thought we had better turn around and head back to the base. By then, the water had become very choppy, tossing the little rowboat all over the place. We tried to put two people in the rowing position, but while we were getting into position, we lost an oar overboard. With only one oar we had no chance.

The choppy water turned into swells and the little boat was going in this direction, then in that direction and we had no control. It was hang on for dear life. We could no longer see the base or Monkey Island. The three of us were at the mercy of the sea. We were not even joking around now. We realized we were in a pretty bad situation.

A Japanese fishing boat passed by us. We screamed and screamed but they never saw us or heard us. We were on a wild ride but it wasn't fun. It was scary! We had no idea in what direction we were heading or in what direction we wanted to go. We could not see land in any direction; we just hoped that the waves would bring us in to land somewhere.

Then we saw it. A light. We were being pushed toward a light that was on land and we didn't care where it was. We were hanging on as the land got closer and closer. The brutal waves were going to throw us ashore and we were hoping it would be nice and easy like. Ha!

A huge wave lifted the boat and threw us against a cement-like breaker, smashing the boat into pieces and stranding us up on the breaker. We were soaking wet, a little banged up, but alive. We didn't know exactly where we were, but we were glad to be there.

It turned out to be a little fishing village, a place that Marines going on liberty would never go. We asked the residents if they would please call the base, but that didn't get through to them. We then asked them to call the Japanese police. That they understood.

The base was notified and a vehicle was dispatched to pick us up, along with the remaining pieces of the rowboat. We were read the "riot act" for being stupid enough to try to row out to Monkey Island. One officer even suggested that we should pay for the rowboat! We didn't, of course. But it was the last time in my military career that I was in a rowboat.

One of the missions of the Marines at Yokosuka was manning the anti-aircraft guns for the base. There were 2- milimeter pom pom guns and quad 50-caliber machine guns. When I arrived there, I knew nothing about these weapons, but I was assigned as a gun captain because I was a corporal.

A couple of times per month, the guns were dispatched to various locations around the base, and we would track airplanes in and around the area. When Col. Chapman arrived on the scene, he sent us all up in the mountains above Tokyo, where we endured a week of live firing exercises. It really was fun firing the quad fifties. It wasn't long after that training that the weapons were removed from the base. The word was that Col. Chapman didn't want them there.

One thing the colonel *did* want was inspections and parades. Once a month, he had a special inspection and parade for the Japanese security guards and their guard dogs. We would look out the window at Marine barracks as they passed in review. Then someone said, "All dogs not actually on watch will stand this inspection." That got to be the cry in the barracks.

The colonel also established a "measured post" to be walked during every inspection and parade day. A Marine walks a "measured post" when he wears dress blues and paces back and forth outside the colonel's office door. The actual post is no more than 10 or 15 steps, but it is manned as long as the inspection and parade are in progress. The Marine assigned to walk the measured post maneuvers his rifle into different positions using very formal, choppy movements. To watch the Marine on that post, you would think he was a toy soldier. I never had that job

The Marine Corps mascot is a bulldog. Col.Chapman made sure that Marine barracks had a bulldog. A Marine was assigned daily to walk the dog around the base. It was a four-hour shift, and you were allowed to wander anywhere, it didn't matter where. I had this assignment once. My shift was from 1200 to 1600 hours. As I was walking around the base with the dog, I noticed that the Benny Decker Theater was showing a matinee movie. I took the dog into the movie. Everyone knew about the bulldog, so no one questioned me when I took him in. It was an easy four-hour assignment. I don't know what happened to the bulldog. He just kind of disappeared. I didn't know why, and like everyone else, I didn't care.

I always wanted a Marine Corps ring. Back in the States, they cost too much, but I was shocked that the base exchange was selling them for only $1.50. I wore the ring for a couple of days but was short of money so I took my ring to the pawn shop in town. I was surprised that they gave me 1800 yen ($5.00) for the ring. On my next payday, I bought a hand full of rings—Marine, Navy, Army, and Air Force—and made the rounds of pawn shops. It was a good deal, but the exchange never re-stocked them.

We were issued ration cards for liquor. I think the ration was only for 8 or 10 bottles per month. When you were short on money and your ration card was not used up, you could stand in front of the EM club where you would be approached by a Japanese man asking if your liquor card was still good. If it was still good, he would pay you 1800 yen ($5.00) and give you money to buy a bottle, using your ration card. A quick exchange and you got money for the night.

American dollars could not be used in Japan. We were paid in military script. In town the Japanese only accepted the Japanese yen. The reason the Japanese would not accept script was because every once in awhile, the military changed the script. When they did this, the base would be locked down, with no one allowed in or out until the exchange was completed. Once the base was locked down, each person had to turn over all the script in his possession, or, if he lived in town, the exact amount of script in his house. The change was always a surprise, and it caught the Japanese black market off guard. When the base was opened up again after the exchange, all the old script in one's possession was worthless.

I remember a Marine Corps birthday ceremony that we attended. We were in dress blues with all the base "big wheels" in attendance. There were the usual speeches and salutes to the Corps. We had been drinking and getting bored with all the speeches, so we threw some pie at the big wheels and ran out of the hall. They never knew who threw the pie. Then the three of us headed for town.

The bar we entered was jammed with sailors. A western band was playing. We thought, *This is the Marine Corps' birthday, so they should play the* "Marine Corps Hymn." The three of us went to the stage and stopped the music. We told the band to play the "Marine Corps Hymn." I really thought that we would never get out of this bar alive. Then the band played the "Marine Corps Hymn" and we sang. By the way, none of us could carry a tune. We sang loud, and actually were surprised when the sailors sang along. They applauded us as we left the stage and the bar. It was at this moment that I made my mind up that I would not go out on liberty with them again. It was fun while it lasted, but no good could come from it. I told the amigos and they just laughed. I told them if I was going to get into trouble it would be my doing, not because I had to support those guys. I never went on liberty in Japan with them again! Both Cpl. H and Cpl. S left Japan as PFCs. I left on the promotion list for sergeant..

Robert S. was the first to leave Japan. His enlistment was almost up and he was not going to re-enlist. He did, however, want to remain in Japan as close as possible to his release date. He had a plan and asked me to help.

He had his orders sending him to a Navy barracks for temporary housing until transportation could be arranged for him. He removed the first page on the order and went out in town to have a duplicate page made with new dates but still sending him to temporary housing. The Japanese printer also duplicated the "ORIGINAL" stamp that had to be on the first page of orders in order for them to look authentic. The problem was that when he picked up the new duplicated top page, he didn't notice that the word ORIGINAL was misspelled. The Japanese printer spelled it "ORIGINIAL."

I was going to forge the Adjuant's signature on the orders. When Robert S. saw that misspelled word, he said, "The hell with it It's too late now and nobody will notice it. I'll take my chance. I did my best forgery." He went telling everybody goodbye.

He remained hidden in the temporary housing, coming out only in the evening and when the other section of Marines were on duty. They didn't even know him. All went well as he stalled until he had just enough time to go to the States and be released from service.

When the new colonel showed up, he came with his dog! The colonel didn't like anything. When he held inspections he brought his dog with him. It was a small dog, I didn't even know what breed. We had to stand there at attention while he and his piss ass dog walked all over our shoes. When we held barracks inspections, the dog would wonder all over the barracks.

The colonel always found something wrong, no matter what we did. After awhile, we used to leave cigarette buts on the floor, almost out in the open, so the colonel and his dog would find it and go away. He never said anything complimentary, so we let him find something unsatifactory right away, so he would make a lot of noise and then he gone. When Col. Chapman left, everyone knew he would be the commadant some day but this colonel wouldn't make a good dog catcher

When we had our clothing inspection, this new colonel was pissed off because we all had new underwear, new socks, new shirts, new belts, new shoes, and new ties. The reason we had all new clothes was because we had so many of this type of inspection, we called the inspections "junk on the bunk" or "things on the springs." New clothes were easy to place out on the bunk.

Folding everything in the proper way took time, and marking all the clothes with your name exactly in the correct spot took even more time, so almost everyone had a duplicate set of clothes that he never wore. These clothes were stashed away in your foot locker and only surfaced for inspection. Laying out the clothes that were already folded and marked properly made it simple. He wanted to see what we actually wore. Colonel Chapman almost demanded new clothes. If you put out something that you actually wore he would find a worn spot and chew you out for not having serviceable clothes.

But orders for me arrived and I was going home. I left the States in November 1952 and now I'm returning in 1956. Destination: Camp Lejeune, North Carolina, for my second tour, via the Bronx, New York!

CAMP LEJEUNE
1956 - 1957 (2ND TOUR)

Back again at Camp Lejeune, NC, nothing changed. It looked just the same. I reported in and was assigned to another rifle company. I made up my mind right then and there that I was not going to stay a here for a full tour. Camp Lejeune duty was not for me. I wanted to go back overseas.

My plan to go back overseas was very simple. I went into the first sergeant's office and requested a transfer. He laughed. "There is no way you can get out of here before two or three years," he told me. I asked if I could put in a request to Marine Corps Headquarters in Washington DC. He said not a chance! Then he said the only place I would be going was to Viequez in a couple of weeks.

Viequez again! I thought, *This will be my third trip down there.* The battalion packed up and we were trucked to Morehead City, NC, to board ship. We boarded an aircraft carrier converted for Marine Corps helicopter squadrons. We were going to make a helicopter assault on Viequez. I was on the sergeant's promotion list, but not yet picked up. I could use the extra money!

The island looked the same as it had before—beautiful green hillside and white sandy beaches. It was dawn when we made our assault on the Island. My fire team was in the second wave of helicopters. I was carrying a wooden box of land mines (duds). In the helicopter, I was sitting facing the doorway, making me the third man to exit when we touched down. As we landed, the first person out was our squad leader. He would stay by the door 'til the helicopter was empty, then give a thumbs up to the pilot. That was the signal that it was okay to lift off. The second man was now out and I was on my feet moving toward the exit, when all of a sudden the helicopter took off, throwing me right out of the helicopter. I landed on my face. I was airlifted back to the ship, spent a couple days resting, and then sent back to my unit. I suffered cuts and bruises and a good black eye.

What happened was that our pilot saw someone giving a thumbs up and thought it was from his helicopter. I don't recall any exercise that I have been involved with that has been free of accidents. I guess you could say that's the cost of doing business in the Marine Corps.

We stayed on the island for about a week and then made our way to the Panama Canal zone. We were going to play some war games in the jungle. It was my first and last trip to Panama. I can't say to much about it because we saw nothing but jungle. And the jungle was something else. It was so thick that if you ventured off the beaten path ten yards, you found yourself in darkness in the middle of the day. We played the game for a couple of days, then boarded ship and headed home.

On the way back to Camp Lejuene, a new idea popped into my mind about how to get back overseas. I remembered that Col. Chapman had told all of us during his farewell speech in Yokosuka, Japan, that if we had a problem or needed something, he would try to help. Was he just saying that or did he really mean it? Would I be breaking the chain of command by going directly to a colonel? I thought a lot about it and decided to take the man at his word and take a chance.

I wrote a letter asking the colonel if he could help me to get back overseas—I didn't care where. I told the colonel about how the first sergeant had not even allowed me to submit a request through regular channels. I wasn't sure if the colonel even remembered me, but I hated the thought of staying at Camp Lejeune for another two or three years, so I gave it a shot.

After we were back at Camp Lejeune, we resumed our training program. Then one day, I got the letter I was waiting for. In the letter Col. Chapman said that if I put my request in before May 15th (it was now the middle of April) that I would be on a draft for overseas assignment. He also said that I should show this letter to the first sergeant if he refused to submit my request.

I took a deep breath and entered the first sergeant's office. I requested permission to submit an application for transfer for an overseas assignment. He blew his top again. I let him say his peace, then showed him the colonel's letter. He was fuming. He turned bright red with rage. He told me that he would do everything in his power to get this request turned down. He went into the captain's office for his endorsement, which was negative. The first sergeant then told me that the request would go through the chain of command, and when one disapproved it, all would disapprove it.

A couple of weeks later, I was called into the first sergeant's office. He told me that they needed a sergeant for drill instructors' school and guess who just volunteered. I thought the SOB got me. I wanted no part of drill instructors' school at Parris Island, SC. He said my orders were being prepared . Then, a funny thing happened. I was recalled by the first sergeant. When I went into his office, he was mad as hell and bright red.

It seems that my orders for going overseas came in: an immediate transfer to the 1st Marine Brigade in Hawaii. I quickly checked out of the battalion and the company, picked up my orders and travel pay, and was gone. My time at Camp Lejeune was short, and I couldn't get out of there fast enough!

HAWAII
1957 - 1959

I reported to Travis Air Force Base in California for transportation to the island of Ohau in Hawaii. While waiting around Travis for a couple of days, I met another Marine going to Hawaii. He was a sergeant, named Mac. Well, Mac and I became buddies because we were the only two Marines on this base. We tried our hand at bowling and got hooked on it. During the days we waited, we spent all our time bowling, and I mean every minute of every day. We were both terrible bowlers but it was fun.

Our flight to Hawaii was uneventful. When we arrived, the 1st Marine Brigade was out in the field and we were told to just hang around for a couple of days, that they would be returning shortly. So it was back to the bowling alley while we waited. I think one night we bowled 'til dawn.

When the brigade returned, we were assigned to different companies. Our bowling career was put on hold. The only difference between the brigade in Hawaii and the division in Camp Lejeune was that Hawaii is a tourist hot spot. In Camp Lejeune when you went on liberty to Jacksonville, the closest town, you walked the streets shoulder-to-shoulder with Marines all looking for the same thing. At Camp Lejeune you stayed on the base more than going out. In Hawaii that's wasn't the case. Tourists were all over the place and your odds improved nightly.

Mac and I bought an old (and I do mean *old*) car for $25. It could not pass the base inspection for a base sticker, so we left it outside the main gate. The car was an Hornet. It had no side windows, no windshield wipers, questionable breaks, and bald tires. But what could we expect for $25.

Now the road going into Honolulu was called the Pali. This road snaked over a mountain and down into Honolulu. At the top of the Pali it always rained, and the road coming back down the mountain was subjected to such terribly strong winds that cars driving against them were almost completely stopped in their tracks. At the summit, legend has it that King Kamehameha was causing the winds, and the stronger the winds, the more upset he was. I think you can guess what that legend meant to a bunch of Marines!

The car didn't last long but we drove it like hell 'til it stopped. We would load up the car with all who wanted to go into Honolulu and head for the Pali. We could have avoided the Pali and taken the long way around, but that's not the Marine way. Over the Pali we would go. I drove. Mac didn't have a license, so he would sit in the shotgun seat helping me see as we went over the Pali with the rain beating down. The road had more curves than a snake and without wipers it was difficult to see the curves. Believe it or not, Mac would hang out the window as would the people in the back seat, and all of them would yell when I should turn. It was a riot, but very exciting, and we always made it. We would pat the dashboard and say, "Good girl, good girl," when we got to Honolulu.

The old car broke down and we couldn't afford to fix it up so we sold it. We got our $25 back. With the $25, we rented a new Oldsmobile for the weekend. We drove that new Oldsmobile all over the island, making sure we got our money's worth. The trip over the Pali was entirely different with a car that had wipers, tires, brakes, and all its windows.

Going to the fields in Hawaii was different. They had lots of mountains in Hawaii, and of course that's where the training exercises would be held. We made landings on different islands, playing war games. When up in the hills, we were always looking down on the pineapple fields, which were 100% off limits. There was a $50 fine if we were caught taking a pineapple from the field. We were out in the field eating c-rations and not getting any fruit our diet. What would you do? After dark we sneaked down into the pineapple fields and helpd ourselves.. Fresh pineapple tastes great!

I was surprised one day, when John H., one of the original three amigos, came into the sergeant's quarters. He just reported in and I remembered that I had told him that I would not go on liberty with them in Japan. He asked, "How about in Hawaii?" We had a good laugh. I was really glad to see him because we got along so well.

One day, John told me that in his company there was a sergeant trying to sell a very nice Chevy, that he wanted to buy it but didn't have a license. He said he would buy it if I would teach him how to drive. I agreed. Every day I would take him out of the way of any traffic and teach him how to drive. I wasn't a good teacher because he failed his driving test twice.

I would keep the car at my barracks. After working hours I would drive over to his place and out to Honolulu we would go. We found a local bar that we liked and after awhile, the locals even liked us. Usually locals didn't like servicemen coming into their bars but I guess they thought we were harmless. Finding a nice local bar was great. All the servicemen, headed for the honky-tonk bars on Hotel Street. Drunks and fights were no longer our calling. We drank and ate quietly and enjoyed it.

Someone somewhere must have looked at my personnel record because all of a sudden I was transferred to MCAS (Marine Corps Air Station Kanohe Bay). It was the same base, but I was no longer in the 1st Marine Brigade.

I was stationed with the base police or "base guard" as they called it. Base guard was the same as the military police except we had jurisdiction only on the base. The living quarters were better here because their sergeants' quarters had actual beds with big mattresses and night stands and lounge chairs. As far as I was concerned, this was the top of the line. My assigned duty was sergeant of the guard. When assigned to this duty, one was in charge of the guard for the day. There was an officer of the day but it was the sergeant of the guard who actually set the guard roster.

A new guard came on duty every morning at 8 o'clock. The new sergeant of the guard would march the color guard from the guard house to the base flag pole for morning colors. At exactly 8 a.m., colors would be sounded. At the end of colors, all personnel all around the base would face the colors and salute (if they were in uniform) or stand at attention (if they were not in uniform).

One morning after I was relieved by the new sergeant of the guard, I headed back to the sergeant's quarters to get some sleep. I heard the sound of colors as I laid my head down on my pillow. All of a sudden someone was shaking me, shouting, "Sergeant Landry! Sergeant Landry, get dressed! Get up!" It was the major in charge of the security section. I jumped up and asked what was going on.

He told me that I was the only sergeant in the quarters and that I had to relieve the sergeant of the guard immediately. He told me to look out the window. The flag had been raised upside down! The major was panicking. "Hurry! Hurry and relieve Sergeant S. now!" I went back on duty for another 24 hours. I learned a lesson that day: when you're off duty, get the hell out of there; don't hang around!

Some days when you are the sergeant of the guard you have nothing to do and you are just putting in your time. Other days you haven't got a minute's rest. This particular day started off like a normal, not-to-busy day, but it turned out to be anything but normal. At about three or four o'clock in the afternoon there was a severe auto accident with fatalities. It had been a head-on crash. I responded to the scene. It wasn't a pretty sight. As soon as I arrived at the scene, my radio blurted out a call that an aircraft had crashed while practicing touch-and-go landings on one of the two runways on the station.

The base now had sirens going off at the airstrip and an ambulance heading for the head-on collision. Then the third emergency call sounded: another plane was having problems and the runway had to be prepared for a possible crash landing. He made it down okay. What a day to be sergeant of the guard. The officer of the day and I earned our pay that day!

Every time a Marine is relieved of duties, he has to clear his weapon and turn it in. To clear your weapon, you release the magazine, pull the slide to the rear, look in the chamber to make sure there is not a round in the chamber, release the slide forward, and fire the weapon into a sand-filled barrel.

I happened to be standing by the sergeant of the guard's desk when a Marine sergeant came in to turn in his pistol after being relieved from duty. As he entered the guard shack he pulled the trigger and BOOM went the gun. The round zipped past my head into the wall. He never released the magazine before he pulled the slide to the rear, and when he released it forward, it put a round into the chamber. When he pulled the trigger you know what happened. He pleaded with me not to report the incident, but his pleas were falling on deaf ears. He got off easy; he only lost a stripe, but he could have killed someone and that someone would have been me.

I have been told that I snore. All the sergeants in our quarters say so. I told them I sleep like a baby and I didn't know what the hell they were talking about. One day at a company formation the major called me front and center. I had no idea what this was about. When I got front and center he read a letter from another major to me. The subject of the letter was snoring. He said that my snoring had caused the proficiency of the sergeants' duties to deteriorate because of a lack of sleep. He said that I had been known to empty an entire movie theater with my snoring and he ended with an order to cease snoring immediately. When he presented me the letter the entire company broke up laughing and applauding. The company was having a little fun at my expense. By the way, my wife keeps telling me I snore!

When the infantry units went on field exercises on different islands, they used us as MPs. This time we went to Hawaii, the big island. We were billeted in Hilo. We had walking patrols throughout the city. In the guard office there was a telephone, which we all used it to make local calls. Then one day someone found out that we could use the phone to make long distance calls without having to pay.

I wasn't aware that long distance calls were being made. I knew that they were using the phone for local calls and that was all right. The call came from the Hawaiian Telephone Company supervisor. The supervisor told me that a significant number of long distance calls had been made from our phone and that the bill was awfully high. "Who is going to pay for these?" she asked. We received a list of calls made and had all the troops pick out the calls they made. All liberty was cancelled for the offenders until they paid their bill.

Someone in the Marine Corps (I don't know who or why) made the decision to revise the enlisted rank structure. They slipped in a new E3 rank called "lance corporal" and pushed all above ranks up a notch. The result was that you didn't get promoted to the new ranks; your title just changed to "acting."

I became an "acting" sergeant E4, because the new rank structure gave a sergeant an E5 pay grade and I was only an E4. It kind of became a joke that everybody was "acting" until the actual new rank promotions came out. The only rank that actually benefitted from this change was the existing E7 master sergeant or 1st sergeant. They automatically moved up to the E8 and /or E9 position. Who said the Marine Corps was fair!

One day I was called into the major's office and told that I had been accused of discrimination. At the time, I had eight black Marines assigned to my platoon and one of them filed charges against me. He claimed that I deliberately picked on him because of his color. The major told me that he would have to investigate the charges.

The major interviewed all the other members of the platoon, who affirmed that the Marine who accused me was a lazy goof off and that I never had discriminated against any of them. Charges were dropped! By the way, that Marine who accused me of discrimination was arrested by the Honolulu police two weeks later on a rape charge. I never knew what had happened to him because my orders came in assigning me to Sasebo, Japan.

Before leaving for Japan I purchased a car from another Marine sergeant (I mean an *acting* sergeant). This time I paid $600 for a red Lincoln Capri with a black hardtop. I think it was 1953 or 1954. The $600 came from my re-enlistment bonus for six more years in the Corps. The orders for Japan were a great surprise and I was delighted. I found out that pay grade E4s could ship their cars to Japan via the government. I made the proper arrangements and caught a flight out of Hickam Air Force Base. As my plane lifted off and flew over the sandy beaches of Hawaii, I realized that in the two years I spent on the island of Oahu, I never once went to the beach!

SASEBO, JAPAN
1959 - 1962

"Prepare for landing," we were told. The long flight from Hawaii to Tokyo, Japan was coming to an end. We were about to touch down when all of a sudden the plane took off. No one told us anything. This was an Air Force plane, not a commercial plane. We circled the air strip and again went in for a landing. Just as we touched down, the pilot took off again, and this time we did not circle; we clearly left the area. Finally someone came back and told us that there were extremely heavy winds and that we could not get down. We flew to the air base at Atsugi and landed safely. A bus took us to temporary quarters overnight. In the morning I received a travel voucher for the Japanese train to Sasebo, and a bus ride to the Tokyo train station. Sasebo was about 840 miles from Tokyo, and in those days, that meant a 24-hour trip!

We had to change trains when we reached the city of Fukuoka, which was about an hour outside Sasebo. It was a long and slow journey. I was glad to see the name Sasebo on the station as we pulled in. Japan had not changed much since the last time I had been there. I was in a different town, around new people, but everything was the same. I had to wait at the station for a vehicle from the base to come and pick me up. I had gotten used to waiting, so another hour or so didn't make much difference. I had used up all my yen for food on the train and only had 150 yen (roughly .50 cents) in my pocket. I was hungry. I bought a bowl of rice, threw on a little soy sauce, and was very happy.

The base at Sasebo was smaller than the base at Yokosuka. The Marine barracks was not a spit-and-polish post. Here everyone was more relaxed. I heard that some people called it a country club. That became clear to me as I checked in. The first question I was asked was, "What sports do you play?" I was assigned to the provost marshal's office to work at the pass and tag office.

73

The provost marshal's office and the pass and tag office was in a building called the CP building. It was off the base. It was the first time in my Marine Corps career that I had to drive to work. The CP building was a Japanese Naval building during the war. In the pass and tag office we issued license tags for US military forces vehicles and base passes for civilians workers. Some of the workers were permanent and were issued a permanent pass. We changed them yearly. Other workers received a temporary pass.

The Marine I replaced took me on a tour of the building, introducing me to different department heads. When he was showing me the labor office, I asked him about one of the Japanese girls working there. He told me to forget about her, that she would have nothing to do with Americans. Forgetting about her was hard to do—she was beautiful!

The provost marshal was on the second floor of the building. My boss, Sergeant L., was the senior criminal investigator for the base. He had three Japanese investigators working for him. I used to ask them to put in a good word for me with that beautiful girl in the labor office. They told me that her name was Masako and that she doesn't date. But I kept on asking.

One day I was at the exchange and I picked up a bunch of hamburgers and brought them to the office. I took them upstairs to the investigators, as a sort of bribe, and again asked about Masako. One of the investigators was on the phone while I was making my pitch. When he hung up the phone he turned to me and said, "She will be here in a minute." The door opened and there she was, even more beautiful standing so close. In Japanese she asked the investigators what they wanted. They told her that I wanted to talk to her. She turned and looked at me with that what-do-you-want look. I was speechless but I picked up the hamburgers and asked if she would like one. She said, "No thank you," made a slight bow and left. It was the beginning. As of this writing we have been married 41 years.

The new promotion list came out and I was promoted to sergeant again, this time as an E5. In the barracks there were maybe 11 sergeants with an E4 rank and I was the only sergeant with an E5 rank. The executive officer of the barracks called me into his office and congratulated me on my promotion. He then said that he really didn't know what to do about my promotion. You see, I was not staff sergeant E5, only a sergeant E5. Not being a staff NCO, I was not allowed to move into the staff's quarters. The captain did give me the staff privilege of being able to exit the base without checking in or out, and not having to use a liberty card.

The sergeant major of the barracks got hooked on bowling. He bowled every day and sometimes would call me at the pass office and ask me to meet him at the alley during working hours to bowl. I told the sergeant major that I could not leave the pass office during working hours. I was the only one authorized to sign any pass issued. My boss, SSgt L,. asked me to join his bowling team. It was mixed couples with a fifth bowler of either sex. They bowled on Friday night and I was an extra. He had a fifth bowler but needed me in case the fifth member of the team could not bowl.

Ever since Hawaii, I have enjoyed bowling. As I grew up in my family, my older brother was the bowler. I was never at his level but I was pretty good. The base was forming a bowling team to go to Tokyo and enter the Armed Forces Far East Championship. To pick the team, there would be a 15-game bowl off, with the top 10 contestants making the team.

When it was all said and done, I slipped in at the number 10 spot. I beat out a Navy Officer who was the boss of that beautiful girl working in the labor office. Because we both worked in the same building, we would bump into each other once in awhile, but he was never friendly after he found out that I was going out with her.

As the NCO in charge of the pass office, I had many visitors, all trying to get me to give them a pass to come on the base to sell their goods. The laundry truck companies were the worst. They lobbied hard to get that sticker for their trucks. One day I had a visitor from one of the laundry companies. Through my interpreter he said he just wanted to welcome me to Japan and he hoped that I enjoyed my stay.

After he left I noticed an envelope laying on my desk. I opened it and it was packed with money! I took it upstairs to my boss, SSgt. L. He kind of laughed and said he would take care of it. I learned later that his taking care of it meant it went into his pocket!

Masako and I were going out for about a year we decided to get married. Now getting married to a Japanese national if you are in the United States military is a problem. You have an awful lot of red tape to overcome. They wanted the life history of the Japanese national's family. The Japanese have such a document, called a "Koseki Tohon." Then there were all the forms that had to be filled out and all the interviews I had to go through. It was a stall tactic that had many people just giving up. We didn't give up. It took a while to get married, and in the end, we ended up getting married three times. We had to satisfy the Japanese government so that I could have my name put on Masako's family history. Then we had to satisfy the United States government, which meant getting a certificate from the U. S. Embassy. And finally, we had to satisfy the church requirements. The end result was we were officially married in the eyes of the Japanese government, The United States government and the Catholic Church.

The Base bowling team went off to the Armed Forces Far East Bowling Tournament in Tokyo with new blue blazer jackets and high hopes. The team consisted of six Navy men and four Marines. We didn't stand a chance. One of our members was in contention for overall score during the tournament but ended up in third place. As for the rest of us, it was a nice trip and a lot of fun.

During the softball season, the base went crazy. All the games were played at night and everybody attended the games. It was the thing to do in the summer. I was approached to manage one of the two Marine Corps teams. The Marines have two teams entered each year. The Navy would not let us combine and have one team, so the barracks was split in half, with one side becoming the red team and the other side, the gold. I became the playing manager of the red team. I was a catcher and a pretty good hitter. I was a contact hitter, very rarely striking out.

I remember the first time I was stationed at Camp Lejeune. There were tryouts for the Regimental baseball team. I signed up for the tryouts. There were a zillion guys out there, all trying to get out of some sort of work. I lingered in the outfield, shagging fly balls, with a large number hanging across my chest. They would call you by number to the batting cage. I waited for what seemed like forever, and never heard my number called.

It was going to be dark soon and I would have never gotten a chance. I walked over to the manager of the team and his staff and told them that I had just been told that I had an emergency phone call at the barracks. He asked me if I had been in the batting cage and when I said no, he told me, "Get in there before you go." You can wait for things to happen or you can make things happen. I took swings in the batting cage and as soon as I finished I was called over to the staff and told what time we would meet tomorrow and where to go for uniforms and equipment.

Our softball season was rolling along. We were the talk of the base, not because of me, but because of our first baseman. He could hit the ball a mile. Almost every other time up, he hit it out of the park. My job was easy—let him do his thing. We also had a speedster. He could run like a deer. And run he did. I just caught and let them play ball.

Masako had a hard time during her pregnancy with Frances. She could hardly eat, as everything wanted to come back up . As the time approached, we went to the hospital often. Each time they told us to go home and relax, that it wasn't our time yet. It was in the middle of the night and we had to go to the hospital. Again the doctor on duty told us to go home.

In the morning I called the head of the hospital who had been taking care of Masako all along. I told him what happened and he told me bring her right back. The baby was born premature and had to remain in an incubator for a week after birth. She was a beautiful baby girl we named Frances.

When we took her home from the hospital, we had no idea what to do. Masako could not breast feed her so we prepared the bottles. She just screamed and screamed as we tried to give her that first bottle, because she was not getting any milk from the bottle. We didn't know what to do so we knocked on a neighbor's door. They gave a simple answer: there is a stopper that must be removed before giving the bottle to the baby. Then the feeding began!

It was a big game! The hospital team and Marines were strong rivals. The stands were over-packed with standing room only. In the first inning, with the hospital up and a man on third with one out, the batter hit a fly ball to left field. The outfielder caught the ball and the man on third tagged up and headed right at me, for home. The ball and the man almost got there at the same time. I caught the throw and made the tag on the runner. He slid hard and caught me above the ankle with his spikes. Down I went, holding on to the ball for the out. I tried to stand up and fell back down. My leg had been broken in two places. The medical team arrived quickly and fixed a splint while waiting for the ambulance. I was out of the game but my boys won.

I remained at the base hospital for about a week. Then they air lifted me to Yokosuka Naval Hospital, which was a bigger facility, better-equipped to handle certain cases. The doctors said that I would still have to wait about a week before they could operate, because of the swelling. The operation went well. They placed an 8" pin in my leg and a 3 and 1/2 " screw across my ankle. I was out of action for about 6 weeks.

Patients in the ward I was in had all kind of injuries to the legs and/or ankles. Every morning the doctor would make his rounds, seeing all the patients. This was torture time—but not for me because I was in a cast and all the doctor asked was how I was feeling. As for all the people with knee and/or leg injuries not requiring a cast, this was torture time. With the patient lying down, the doctor would pick up his leg as high as he could, and tell the patient to hold it up because he was going to drop it. The patients pleaded with the doctor not to drop their legs. He never listened. The screams were blood curdling. I remember the doctor asking one patient how much flexibility he had in his knee. The patient showed the doctor and told him, "I just can't get anymore flexibility yet." The doctor said, "We'll just have to see about that."

The doctor then sat on the edge of the bed, lifted the man's leg over his shoulder and holding on to the patient's foot, the doctor stood up with the patient's left dangling down the doctor's back, upside down. You should have heard the scream. "What are you screaming about?! It's only pain," the doctor said. I was glad I had a broken leg in a cast.

I was getting along with a wheel chair and could go down to the mess hall for my meals. It was better than staying in bed all day long. The doctor told me that I was being sent back to Sasebo and that meant I could see my wife and daughter again. I was air-lifted back and after a doctor's examination, was sent back to work on light duty. The pass office was light duty anyway.

My car was in the shop while I was in the hospital. I let the Navy attendant at the garage use the car. I called him "Ski." I couldn't pronounce his real name anyway. Ski was a great guy and we had become friends. His wife and my wife got to know each other, because his wife worked at the base chapel office and Masako had been going there, taking lessons in Catholicism so we could be married in the Church. Ski was a guy that could fix and/or build anything. He came over to our house and put in a cement walk and fixed us up with a retractable clothes line. Ski loved kids and always said that he wanted at least nine so he could have his own baseball team. When I came out of the hospital, Ski told me that the car would need a new engine and it would not be worth fixing. I got a couple hundred bucks for it.

I had heard that there was a need for duty managers at the EM club. I went to interview for the part-time job. I got the job and worked a couple of nights a week. As the duty manager, I ran the club after the permanent manager went home. If the crowd was light (because not enough ships were in port), I would determine how many people I needed to keep the bar running, and let the others go for the night. They allowed me a $50 limit to buy drinks and/or dinner for complainers.

I wore a suit and tie and just walked around the club, trying to keep everyone happy. When they had a floor show, I was the master of ceremonies. I used to get a kick out of it because when I came on to introduce the show, I got a huge applause, but when the show was over and I came out to close the show, they booed me off the stage.

The club had slot machines and I had the waitress watching which machine had been played all night but never hit a jackpot. When they came and told me of such a machine, I would put an out-of-order sign on that machine. After we closed for the night I would play. Sometimes it paid off and sometimes it didn't.

I also worked (if needed) as a Bingo caller. I was a substitute caller and worked when the regular caller was not available. Early on in my tour at Sasebo, a buddy of mine and I were dead broke. We pooled our resources and came up with $2.00. We went up to the club on a Bingo night and had a couple of beers and decided to buy one card. The card cost a dollar and that pretty much wiped us out. We sat there through all the games with barely a nibble. But on the last game, called "Blackout," we were in the running, needing only one more number. When they called that number we both jumped up and screamed at the top of our lungs, "BINGO!" It paid $500 and they gave us a check.

We couldn't cash the check, so we went back to the barracks and said that tomorrow we would walk into the executive officer's office and ask for a day off, to celebrate. In the morning we walked into the office and asked for the day off. When he asked why we needed time off, we said we had never won anything like this, and winning $500 is a once-in-a-lifetime event. He told us to go out have fun, but be good.

I had purchased a little Japanese Datsun car. It was an old one but now running like new. When Masako was pregnant with Frances, we took a trip to the exchange at another base. We were picking up another couple that morning when all of a sudden a Japanese taxi slammed into the side of us.

The driver got out and in Japanese, told Masako to say that the American was drunk. Masako told the driver that all I had for breakfast this morning was cereal and coffee, and was *not* drunk. When the Japanese police arrived, Masako relayed the story to them and it was ruled the taxi driver's fault. The car was still operational so we continued on our trip.

Within a couple of days, the cab company wanted to clear up this accident. I told them through one of the provost marshal interpreters that this would not be settled until after my wife delivered and we saw that the baby and my wife were okay. After the birth of Frances, they kept calling and calling, but I just made them wait. Finally, I told them that the car was not running very well and before I signed off on this accident, this car had to run a lot better.

They gave me a loaner car and took the car to their garage. In a few days they called and wanted me to come down to their shop with my interpreter. When we got there they took us to a very large warehouse. In that warehouse, laid out on the floor in some kind of order were all the parts of my car. They completely rebuilt the engine and replaced any and all parts that even *looked* worn. Within the week I had my datsun again running like new!

Bastille Day in France is a big holiday. Here in the United States it's a big day for Masako and I, because on July 14, 1962, our son Brian was born. I had received orders to report to Camp Lejeune, NC, but we could not go because the doctor said that we could not travel with Brian until he is three months old.

At about this time, all transfers and leaves, etc., were put on hold, due to the Cuban Missile Crisis. All our belonging were shipped to the States and I had traded my Datsun for a Plymouth station wagon that had just arrived from the States. The owners, after seeing the small streets here in Japan, didn't want a big car and were glad to trade for the Datsun. On the other hand, a station wagon was what we needed for the drive across the country to New York and then to Camp Lejeune, NC. Somehow I convinced the powers that be that with all our stuff already shipped to the States, we couldn't stay here. I asked the interpreters upstairs in the CP building to make a call to the Japanese government and inquire what was the hold up on Masako's passport.

The reply didn't make me very happy. They said it would probably be about three to four weeks 'til it was processed. Without a passport, Masako could not leave with us. That would mean that I would go alone and whenever the Japanese government sent her passport, Masako would have to travel by herself with two children, ages 14 months and 3 months!

I could not allow that. I asked the interpreters what I could do. They told me there was nothing I could do. I asked where the passport office was and was told it was in Tokyo. I asked them to write down (in Japanese) the address of the passport building in Tokyo. They told me it would be a waste of time to go there. I was on the train the next morning for the two-hour trip to Tokyo.

I got a hotel room in Tokyo and cleaned myself up after that grueling 24-hour ride. I caught a cab and gave the driver the paper with the address of the passport office on it. The building was a typical government building, large and impressive. Inside, all the doors had signs above them in Japanese and English. As I walked down the long hallway, I saw a sign that said "Director of Passports." That's what I was looking for.

Inside, a young Japanese girl was sitting at the receptionist's desk. I asked to see the director but I wasn't getting through to her. It was a language thing. She called someone on the phone motioning me to wait. In came another girl that spoke a little English and I told her I wanted to speak to the director. She asked in broken English if I knew the director. I said he was a *tomodachi* (friend) of mine, a little white lie that got her attention. On another call, in comes a man, this time speaking pretty good English. I explained that I was looking for my wife's passport. He took me upstairs to a large room with four lines of people waiting for the next open window.

I was taken behind the counter and there was a lot of conversation going on in Japanese. I finally made them understand I was looking for my wife's passport. It took awhile, but they produced the passport. I told them that's what I came for. Then the conversation in Japanese began again. In English, they said in two or three weeks! I didn't come to Tokyo to hear that. I told them I wanted it now! More Japanese conversation, hot and heavy, but no movement. I insisted that they give the passport to me now. "Cannot," they said. "Why not?" I replied. We went back and forth, round and round. They finally told me that they could not give it to me because it had to go through the Prefecture (County) Office.

Sasebo was in the Nagasaki Prefecture, so I told them that on my way back to Sasebo, I would stop at the Nagasaki Prefecture Office and get the official stamp that's required. They agreed and the clerk took the passport and made about 4 stamps on different pages and then handed it to me. They also gave me the address the Nakasaki Prefecrure Office. I made my best Japanese bow, smiled and then got the hell out of there with the passport in my hand. The train ride back was less stressful because I had the passport. In Nagasaki the passport people were waiting for me as the Tokyo crew had called ahead and told them to just stamp and give it back to me. We could now leave as a family.

In sales a "no" never means no....it means I just don't know enough of whatever to say "yes." If a sales person takes no for an answer, he or she would not be in business for long. Back at my office, the interpreters were shocked that they gave me the passport. They asked me what I had done and I told them I just refused to take "no" for an answer.

We now had just enough time for Masako and the kids to visit her family in Kure City. The plan was that I would take the train from Sasebo and Masako and the kids would be at the Hiroshima train station waiting. As the train pulled in, she was there with all her family. After a lot of tears and hugs, we were on our way to Yokohama to board a ship back to the United States.

When we got to the pier where the MSTS (Military Sea Transportation Ship) was waiting, we hit another road block. It seems that Brian was missing one of his shots and they would not let us aboard the ship. We had to dart over to a medical facility on the base for the required shot. Once on the ship, we located our cabin and settled down for a two-week trip to San Francisco, California.

The ship was primarily a troop ship. Down below was about a thousand Army soldiers. They were not allowed above the main deck of the ship. Above the main deck was the cabin area. Our cabin had four beds with a bathroom and wash area. Showers and/or baths were just down the hall. The dining room was a couple of decks above and we were assigned a table and a time for eating.

At night there were movies, dances, and a bar. I thought I was the only Marine on the ship, as most of the dependents were Army and Navy. It wasn't a cruise ship, but it was comfortable. I located the area for washing clothes and where we could warm up bottles of milk and sterilize the bottles. Poor Masako—she remained in the cabin most of the time because of the baby. She didn't get along that well with the movement of the ship, either. We hit some bad weather. One day we ran smack into a huge storm. Most of the people aboard the ship were sick. For some unknown reason, the water never bothered me. I had never gotten seasick in my life, and during this storm I just rolled with the punches. I got a big kick out of a couple of sailors traveling with their dependents. They got sick as hell. They had always been stationed on shore duty.

During the storm I didn't miss a meal. I brought food back for Masako and some crackers for the kids to munch on. The kids handled the storm okay. We didn't get out of our cabin at night because we couldn't leave the kids alone, but during the day, I would take Frances for a walk around the ship.

We had been at sea a long two weeks by the time we sailed into Anchorage, Alaska, for a day. I wanted to take Masako and the kids ashore to feel solid ground under their feet, but I couldn't. Her passport stated very clearly that she could only set foot on land at San Francisco, CA. Rules are rules, so we didn't go ashore.

One day out of San Francisco, there was a knock on the door of our cabin. When I opened the door, a man said, "I understand that you are a Marine." When I said yes, I was a Marine, he said he was too, and that we were the only Marines aboard this ship. Today, he said, was November 10th, and if we would come to his cabin, we would drink a toast to our Corps. He was a master sergeant and we had a couple of drinks to celebrate the Marine Corps' birthday.

Everyone was on deck as we approached the Golden Gate Bridge. As we sailed under her the people walking on the bridge were waving like mad. It was a great feeling to be home again! Once we tied up at the dock, we had to wait to get processed to get off. The lines were long and I thought it was going to take forever.

And then I heard someone yell, "MARINES OVER HERE!" A Marine corporal had just come aboard to process Marines, and since there were only two us, we were off the ship in a flash. As a matter of fact, the corporal drove us to the Marine Memorial Hotel in San Francisco where we stayed the night.

In the morning, I headed down to the Union Square Garage where my car had been shipped. They had an agreement with the Navy to handle cars being shipped into California to be picked up by dependents. While in Japan, I had sent them their form, used to request services prior to pick up. I had wanted a complete tune-up, oil and lube, check brakes, front end alignment, and wash.

When I arrived at the garage, the car hadn't been washed. I asked them if the things I asked for had been done and they assured me they were. They told me that in doing the tune-up, the carburetor needed to be replaced and they took care of it. I paid the bill and drove back to the hotel to pickup Masako and the kids.

We headed south to the San Jose area, and after a few days, continued down to L.A. Finally we took off, heading for New York. About a couple of hours out of L.A., the car had problems. The mechanic in the garage told us that the carburetor was no good. I explained to him that it was brand new with only a few 100 miles on it. He pulled it apart and said it was *not* a new carburetor!

The Union Square Garage knew that people like me, when we picked up our cars, would never come back, so they could do what they wanted and tell us anything. I purchased another carburetor. It took a couple of hours for them to pick one up, then we continued on our trip across the country. I did, however, write a letter back to the Navy base in Sasebo, Japan, to the officer in charge of shipping cars and personnel effects back to the States. I told him what happened to me and advised him to warn others before they ship their cars. I hope that company lost some business because of my letter.

In the station wagon, the back seat was laid out flat to allow a place for the kids to walk or play or sleep. It was also easy for Masako to change diapers as we drove. The trip was really uneventful. It was long, taking us about six days. We drove 500 miles a day, stopping every night at a motel We got a good night's sleep, some hot food , a refreshing shower, and in the morning, we were ready to go again.

The plates we were driving on were Japanese plates. There was numbers of course, but also some Japanese writing. At one gas station we stopped at, we told the attendant to fill 'er up. He didn't say anything but when we paid by cash, he remarked that he was worried about how to write the Japanese characters on the sales slip!

As we rolled down the New Jersey Turnpik,e there it was—the New York City skyline! I remember singing out loud, "New York, New York...what a wonderful town...the Bronx is up and the battery is down... the people ride in a hole in the ground." They must have known we were coming because here came the snow!

CAMP LEJEUNE
1962 - 1965 (3ᴿᴰ Tour)

Back Again! At Camp Lejeune, NC, nothing ever changes. It looks the same. I reported in and was assigned to a rifle company—what a surprise. After checking in I signed up for base housing. There were openings so we got in right away. Tarawa Terrace was the housing area we were given. There were three or four one-level units to a building. These were left over from World War II. We ended up with an end unit. There was a large play area so the kids would have plenty of places to run and play. We were not too happy about the close proximity of the units because I like a little breathing room. Someone told me that you can't live out in town because they have empty units and they won't give you permission.

When I reported in for actual duty, I was informed that I had been selected for a promotion to staff sergeant, pay grade E6. I was assigned to a platoon as platoon leader until a new lieutenant came aboard. Within a week or two, the new second lieutenant joined the company. That pushed me back to my rightful job as platoon sergeant. A new second lieutenant right out of college is a thing of beauty. They know nothing but think they are going to rule the world. My new lieutenant was no exception.

After he was settled in he told me he wanted all our troops out in front of the barracks for an afternoon run at 1300 hours. I said, "Yes sir. They will be there." With the platoon assembled in front of the barracks, the lieutenant came into the platoon office where I was drinking a cup of coffee and he told me that the troops were waiting. I had a little fun with him because he didn't know that I still had a pin and screw in my leg and was not ready for running. I told him that the troops didn't want me to run with them because I might fall down and re-break my leg. Then they would have to assign another platoon sergeant, and that's what they didn't want! He looked at me very puzzled but didn't know what to say. Later he found out why I didn't run!

In the field, after a training exercise, we were all siting around waiting for the trucks to come pick us up. I told my young lieutenant, "Let's move our platoon down by the road." He responded, "They didn't call us down yet," but I convinced him to move the platoon down anyway. Once we were down by the side of the road, when the trucks showed up, we were told to get aboard. That put us back at the barracks before the other platoons, because the trucks had to drop us off before they could go back out to pick up other troops. When the troops know that someone is looking after them by getting them back to the barracks and out on liberty before other troops, the morale is high. The young lieutenant was beginning to learn.

One day while driving around with the family, we saw a sign that said, "NEW HOME SALE! $99 DOWN AND $99 A MONTH." We drove to the model homes to take a look. This was what I wanted—a little breathing room. Back at the barracks, I checked with the base housing and found out that I would need the CG's (commanding general's) approval to move out of base housing and rent or buy a property in town. "How do I apply?" I asked. He told me that as long as there were empty units on base, there would be no approvals. I repeated, "But how do I apply?" I was given the request form, which I filled out and submitted. Within a week I received an approval and bought the new home. It took a few months to actually move in because the home had not actually been built yet..

I learned early in my Marine Corps career that just because someone tells you that you can't it doesn't necessarily *guarantee* that you can't! When I was stationed in Hawaii years before, I wanted to go to Japan on leave. I was told that to travel over to the Far East, I would have to have a passport and travel on a civilian airline. When I found out the airfare was too expensive for me, I asked if I could bum a ride to Japan on a military flight. "No," was the blunt answer. "Can I put in a request?" I persisted. "Sure, but they will turn you down," I was told. I submitted the request. and within two weeks the answer came back—

I was APPROVED. I was getting ready to go somewhere else when I received orders transferring me to Japan! I have said it before and I'll say it again: "No" never means no—it only means, "I don't know enough of whatever to say 'yes.'"

Getting ready for a big inspection had my young lieutenant all shook up. We were having a "Junk on the Bunk" inspection by the battalion commander. Having been involved in so many of these kind of inspections in Japan made me an expert. I told the lieutenant, "Just stay out of the squad bay. I'll handle everything In the morning before the colonel arrives, you can come in." When infantry companies have these kind of inspections, it's mass confusion. In the squad bay, the lieutenant, the platoon sergeant, and the squad leaders will all be moving this, straightening out that, making sure everything is done, and in the end it's a disaster.

I picked one Marine's bunk and placed out everything in the exact position it needed to be in. Then I assigned certain people to take the specific items I assigned them and physically place it on the bunks of their squads, using the model display as the only way things should look. No exceptions. If it didn't look like my model, it was wrong. The squad leader was always correct! I did not go back into the barracks as they finished straightening.

The squad bay consisted of two platoons, each one responsible for cleaning half of the squad bay. Each platoon would assign a couple of men to clean the head and hallways daily. For this inspection, the troops would be standing at attention next to their bunks. The lieutenant and platoon sergeant stood by the door, ready to escort the colonel to their respective sides of the squad bay.

In the morning, I told the lieutenant not to touch anything, so the lieutenant walked up and down the squad bay, looking at the displays but not touching. At the other end of the squad bay, their lieutenant and platoon sergeant were going around moving this and adjusting that. In other words, they were not ready for inspection.

In walked the colonel. The squad bay was called to attention. The lieutenant greeted the colonel, "Good morning, Sir. The first platoon is ready for inspection." The lieutenat led the colonel and I followed along with a note pad. The colonel talked to some of the troops and seemed very pleased with what he was seeing. Upon completion, he turned the lieutenant and said, "Excellent looking platoon, Lieutenant." Then he proceeded to the other side of the squad bay to inspect the second platoon. The lieutenant and I remained by the entrance to the squad bay while the colonel continued his inspection. My platoon remained standing by their bunks, at ease.

When the colonel had finished inspecting the second platoon, he was standing in the middle of their side of the squad bay, talking to their lieutenant. The colonel was shaking his finger at the lieutenant. I nudged my lieutenant and told him that the colonel was not saying, "Excellent inspection" to the other lieutenant. The second platoon failed the inspection and had to repeat the inspection on Saturday. My troops were off on liberty.

The Corps was looking for shooters and I signed up for the try-outs. I had always been a good shooter and a shooting match excited me. I made the regimental shooting team and went TAD (Temporary Additional Duty) to prepare for the shooting matches. Our team looked pretty good after we spent every day for two weeks shooting. The match was to be held at Camp Lejeune, and Marines came from all duty stations. The favorite team was what we called "the big team from Quantico, VA." My buddy (another staff sergeant) and I went to the range one day to watch the big team shoot. We thought we were pretty good, but they were unbelievable. We watched a gunnery sergeant shoot the offhand position at 200 yards.

There is a stool to sit on between shots. He would stand, fire, sit, stand, fire, sit, and on and on. As the target went down, he placed a new round in the chamber, and as the target came up showing a white disk (bulls eye) he repeated the motions. Stand, fire, and sit. And he was doing it in the time it took to write the words..."stand, fire, sit." Now I have to tell you that the offhand position is the hardest position to master, but he made it look easy. My buddy and I just shook our heads.

The reason the big team shooters were so good is that they are permanent members of the team and that is all they do. On the pistol side of shooting, the big team had a captain who won a gold medal in the Olympics in pistol shooting. What chance did our regimental team have? Slim to none! But we had fun.

Upon completion of the shooting match, I returned to my unit to find they had deployed on a med cruise. I was told that the shooters would be flown to Spain to meet the battalion. While waiting for orders to fly to Spain, I received a set of TAD orders to the Naval Academy at Annapolis, MD. It seems they selected certain shooters to go to the Naval Academy to assist the freshman class in qualifying with a rifle and pistol. All freshman classes participate in qualifying with weapons in the summer before classes begin.

Upon arrival at the academy, I met other shooters from various Marine Corps posts, and a meeting was set up for introduction of the program we would be running. The actual firing range was not on the grounds of the academy but the "snapping-in" period of about a week was on the grounds. I was over at the academy for the snapping-in period and gave instructions of correct positions for shooting the rifle. After a few weeks of practicing, they qualified with the rifle one day and with the pistol the next. The freshman were so happy when they qualified; they couldn't thank us enough for our assistance. As for me, my claim to fame is that I taught at the Naval Academy!

When I returned to Camp Lejeune after the TAD orders expired, my unit was still on a med cruise. They needed a staff sergeant over at the infantry training battalion and I was assigned to them. The infantry training battalion was new to me because in my early days at Camp Lejeune this organization did not exist.

The infantry training battalian was a good idea. Now when a Marine comes out of Parris Island, he comes into this infantry training battalion for a period of time to be indoctrinated into being a Marine infantryman. All Marines are riflemen and this training reinforces that duty before new Marines are assigned to a permanent duty station. The training consisted of lectures using mock ups of the actual area the Marine would be using, with explanations showing each step of the exercise. Most of the exercises used live ammunition. Safety was a big concern, because running around with live ammo could present serious problems. The exercise was run without ammo a couple of times so everyone knew what to do, and what position he had to be in. Then with live ammo, we would run it again.

One of the most dramatic exercises was the night demonstration of an actual FPL (final protective line). During this exercise, spectators used to come out for the show. An FPL was when a unit is dug in, protecting their position when under attack.

The platoon was spread out over the line and each man assigned an area of responsibility. For safety reasons, all the positions had stakes in the ground showing the limits of responsibility, and the only area each Marine could fire into. All the ammo used were tracers. Tracers allowed us to see the flight of the bullet. At night it's quite a sight. The exercise begins with a narrator up in a high tower above the FPL, calling for one machine gun to fire a burst, and then another, each showing their range of fire.

Then the narrator would have just the BAR men commence firing, one at a time, and finally he would call all others to fire one at a time. Then the grand finale would start, with one machine gun beginning the firing and then, on cue, others would join in until the entire platoon was firing in their areas of responsibility all at the same time. What a sight. To see it, you would think that anyone attacking in this position could not survive.

I gave a lot of lectures while at the infantry training battalion that would help me later on in my career. I wasn't expecting any orders, but in they came, and to my surprise, they were to Marine Corps Air Station, Cherry Point ,NC. We hired a real estate company to manage our house and keep it rented till we returned. We packed our stuff and moved out.

CHERRY POINT
1965 - 1966

The Marine Corps Air Station at Cherry Point, NC, was about 50 miles up the road from Camp Lejeune. I had no idea why they would send an 0369 infantry unit leader to the air wing! The only thing I could think of was for base security.

Cherry Point was a nice looking base. It was not as big as Camp Lejeune, but more comfortable, because the "Wing Wipers" (as we called them) always lived better than us "Grunts." When checking in, we were assigned base housing immediately, and to our surprise, they were very nice quarters. It was the best base housing we have had. It was a three-bedroom individual home with attached carport. It took about a week before I had to report for assignment, and we used that time to unpack and set up housekeeping.

When it was time to check in, I went into the administration office and there was another gunnery sergeant just reporting in, who was also an 0369 infantry unit leader. The adjutant had said we needed one, but they sent us two! Who said the Marine Corps can't plan things? There was only one opening in the security section and we actually flipped a coin to see who went to security. I lost and was assigned to a headquarters company. I really didn't know what I would be doing, but an assignment was an assignment.

When I checked in at headquarters company, I was assigned as NCO in charge of temporary billeting. There were three barracks that housed people coming into and leaving the base. My job as NCO in charge was to see that these three barracks were kept up in tip top shape and to insure that all Marines coming and going were processed in a timely manner. The "wing wipers" didn't like the idea of a grunt coming in and playing Marine. After all, they were Air Wing and they thought they were special. They weren't special; to me they were just Marines.

And as Marines, I expected— no I demanded—that they act accordingly while in my barracks.

My new boss was a captain and he and I got along very well. These transits had nothing to do during the day except wait. I changed that and had a morning formation and some close order drill, putting their own NCOs in charge. I supervised them at first; it took awhile before their own NCOs actually acted like Marines.

The transit barracks was given an "x" number of dollars for supplies.We actually had to go down to the supply warehouse and, using the allotted dollars, make the purchases for the barracks' upkeep. The money was allotted every three months, and during my first three months, I had no need to use it all. I thought they would roll it over to the next period, but they didn't. What they did was subtract the unused funds from my next allotment.

I blew my top and raised hell. I was told the Marine Corps felt that if we didn't use it, we didn't need it. That was the first and last time that I did not use all the funds, down to the last penny. I purchase anything and everything whether we need it or not, including a nice briefcase for the captain and me to carry important papers concerning the billeting of temporary troops. I found that purchase justifiable.

During our tour at Cherry Point, my wife became very ill. The doctors at the base said that they could not treat her and sent her to the Naval hospital at Portsmouth, VA. My CO told me to take whatever time I needed to take her to the hospital and my kids up to my sister's house in New Jersey. During this time period, I would work a couple of days and then the captain would tell me to take off and get up to the hospital. For about a month, I was taking off every Thursday through Monday. I would come back for a couple of days and then be gone again. I was very grateful to the captain.

When my wife came out of the hospital, I went to pick her up. We then drove to New Jersey to pick up the kids. My wife was not doing too well, because this was right after major surgery. My sister in New Jersey said she would come down to NC. and stay for a week or so, 'til my wife got back on her feet. She was God-sent. I don't know what we would have done without her. Over time my wife got stronger and stronger, and I got orders to report to Camp Pendleton, CA. The Vietnam War was going on at this time and orders to California meant going to Vietnam.

To drive to California with two kids would have been too much for my wife, so we headed up to New Jersey and again, my sister reached her hand out in support. From New Jersey, I drove our car out to California, with my wife and kids planning to fly out after I was settled. The new promotion list was due to be posted, and I was hoping to earn a promotion before leaving for Vietnam.

VIETNAM
1966 - 1967

Camp Pendleton was a huge base. There are different areas well spread out and a sort of little base within the bigger one. Upon checking in, I found out that we were heading for Vietnam. I was joining a new battalion just being formed; I was the third person reporting in. There was the commanding officer, a lieutenant colonel, the sergeant major, then me. The colonel told me I would be the S3 operation chief, and as soon as others arrived, we would need a training schedule. This was new to me because I had never been involved with the S3.

An infantry battalion is broken down to three rifle companies and an H&S Company (H&S standing for Headquarters and Service). In the headquarters section, there was the commanding officer, an executive officer, and the following departments: S1-Administration, S2- Intelligence, S3 -Training & Operations, and S4-Supply.

Within a day or two, a Gunnery Sergeant N. reported in and became the new operations chief in the S3. I was glad to see him. He was an experienced operations chief and I became his assistant. He knew what he was doing. Gunnery Sergeant N. was a wheeler and dealer. He knew what the S3 department needed to be operational. Because we were a new battalion, we had to purchase all our own equipment. The battalion had unlimited purchasing power to get ready for deployment to Vietnam in three months.

I was called into the colonel's office one morning and congratulated for my promotion to gunnery sergeant. I remained as Gunnery Sergeant N.'s assistant. The battalion numbers grew daily and it wasn't too long before we were fully manned. The clock was ticking away as our deployment day grew closer. A new master sergeant reported in and he became the new operations chief!

Gunnery Sergeant N. wasn't happy with that. He told me that we had done all the work, then this guy comes in and takes over. The new master sergeant, along with the operations officer, a major, and a lieutenant officer, flew to Okinawa in advance of the Battalion. They also went into Vietnam for a look around. They would meet the battalion in the Philippines.

With hugs and kisses to the family and kids and tears in everyone eyes, we departed to San Diego, CA, to board ship for deployment to Vietnam. It was an aircraft carrier converted for Marine Corps operations for helicopter assaults.

Life aboard ship is laid back. We did, however, have the troops in classes during the day, and with conditioning hikes up and down the numerous stairs aboard a carrier. Gunnery Sergeant N. told me that when we dock in Hawaii he would be getting off this ship and out of this battalion. (He was still upset with that new master sergeant coming aboard.) It's funny how fast everyone disappears as soon as the ship docks. The officers and staff NCOs have open gate liberty and can wear civilian clothes. The troops cannot leave the ship without checking out and receiving a liberty pass. They must be in uniform.

I wasn't in a hurry to go ashore, but I planned to go later. A lieutenant from one of the line companies aboard, spotted me and asked me if I would assemble the troops on the pier at 1300. He told me he couldn't find another gunnery sergeant anywhere. I told him I would have them assembled at 1300 as requested. I had the Navy personnel pass the message over the loud speaker throughout the ship. At 1300 hours, I called the troops to attention, did an about face, and reported to the lieutenant that the troops were assembled. As I started to leave, the lieutenant asked me if I was going to go with them. I told him, "No, sir. I am heading into town." He took the troops for a run around the docks.

We were in Hawaii about three days with the last two spent putting together an operation order for training in the Philippines. In an operation order, all departments have to submit all the information necessary for them to comply with the original order. Usually there are many mistakes in their report and all mistakes have to be removed and proofread again.

Gunnery Sergeant N. and I were going over the submitted reports and sending some back for corrections. The battalion commander came into our little office and asked Gunnery Sergeant who he knew in Hawaii. Gunnery Sergeant turned with a puzzled look on his face and asked, "Sir?" The colonel said that he had been transferred to the commanding general western Pacific staff here in Hawaii. Gunnery Sergeant N. turned toward me and winked. That night he left the ship. The General and his staff were moving to Okinawa. GySgt N knew his way around!

We left Hawaii and headed for the Philippines. We pulled into Subic Bay a Navy Base in the Philippines. Here we came ashore and were put up in empty old quonset huts. All the Staff NCOs in the battalion were billeted together. These quonset huts were completely empty so we bedded down on the floor. There was no hot water in the shower area; it was cold showers or nothing. Boy, was the water cold! The Philippines are a warm climate country, but their water coming from the mountains was ice cold.

We stayed in the field about two weeks. We trained and trained and then trained again. A good fighting unit is a unit that has been together for a long time. We had only been together for a short time, but our training exercises were intense because of our situation. We were not training for fun but for real.

We left the Philippines and headed for Vietnam waters. We were to relieve the SLF (Special landing Force) on station now off the coast of Vietnam. The SLF is a floating battalion of Marines going up and down the coast of Vietnam, ready to be used if needed anywhere.

On the way, we hit a storm that tossed the ship this way and that way. I was never one to get seasick, but there were an awful lot of kids sick. In the chief quarters where the gunnery sergeants were billeted, we slept in a bed, with a mattress and clean sheets. On this particular morning, I was changing the sheets on my bed when a wave gave the ship a toss that threw me across my bed. When that happened, the middle finger on my right hand got stuck on a sheet that I was tucking in, and the top joint of the finger broke.

I mean that the top joint of the finger went down, and when I pulled it up it would go down again. I went to sick bay and they put a splint on the finger. There I was, walking around with the middle finger on my right hand bandaged with a splint so that my other fingers could not be straighten out. I looked like I was walking around giving everyone the finger.

With our arrival, the existing SLF force moved in country and we took over. This was the beginning of our 13-month rotation. A couple of times we went on alert and were ready to go ashore, but were never called. All in all, for three months we were on a military cruise hip without going ashore. The food was good and the quarters clean and comfortable, and we watched movies every night. Who could ask for anything more?

The three months passed slowly, and upon being relieved we headed in land to place called Dong Ha. Here we moved into a tent city, setting up patrols around the area and awaiting orders. About a week after our arrival, they came. We were heading south, about half way between Dong Ha and Hue. We moved down the road in a large convoy. We were told that this would be a good place for our "Baptism of fire." The word was that there was little or no action in this area. Once we got off the road and into the actual area where we were to set up, things changed, starting that night!

With the battalion setting up a parameter defense, along with artillery support, we settled down, but not for long. We were attacked by a North Vietnamese regular Army unit almost as soon as the sun went down. At first sunlight, there were a large number of North Vietnamese bodies across the front of the battalions line. The next night they came again, and made their final attack on the third night. One North Vietnamese soldier was found alive, and under interrogation said that they were told that we were South Vietnam Marines and that we would fold if attacked.

I guess the rest of the Marine Corps area of responsibility was quiet, because on the 4th day, a lot of reporters were flown in, looking for stories. After those three attacks, the nights became silent. The battalion sent out search and destroy patrols, but found no resistance. The patrols went further and further out, but still found nothing.

The area became almost like a reserve area. Not much of anything was going on, and the only things we were missing were movies and beer. Movies we never got, but beer—that was another story. With the entire battalion coming in-country at the same time, the battalion had to be broken up because they couldn't send the entire battalion home at the same time. A gunnery sergeant reported in from the 12th Marine Brigade and replaced me. I was reassigned to the 12th Marine Brigade at Dong Ha. I had to wait for a convoy heading down to Da Nang to catch a plane or another convoy heading from Da Nang to Dong Ha.

The battalion requested and received permission to hand out two beers per day, per man. The hitch was that they had to send people down to Da Nang to get the beer. Because I was going to Da Nang anyway, I was asked to help get the truck to Da Nang. I picked up a truck and driver along with two additional helpers and we joined a convoy heading to Da Nang. When we got to Da Nang, we found the distributor of the beer. After he checked his list to see that we were authorized to pick up the beer, he told us to come back tomorrow.

We really had no place to sleep, so we went looking for a place to drink. We were told the Army had the best club, and that's where we went. When we got there, the club was almost like a stateside club. We stood, tired and dirty, and shocked to see all these Army dudes in class "A" uniforms, in the middle of Vietnam. All of a sudden we heard a loud voice saying, "MARINES!" A Marine master sergeant came over to us and said, "Always glad to see Marines." I looked at him and was kind of stunned because he was my platoon sergeant from Korea, who I thought was dead!

He was Staff Sergeant E. then, and when I returned from the hospital ship in Korea, I was told he had been killed. He remembered me and we talked about the old platoon. He was a language expert now and assigned to this Army unit. He took us to the mess hall for chow, and found us places to sleep for the night. This Army unit had washing machines, and that night we washed our clothes and after a good night's sleep, we went to get the beer.

At the beer warehouse, we found that the cans were not in cases; they were single cans of beer. I asked the Marine in charge how many cans we could get. He told us, "As many as you can get on your truck!" We backed the truck up and started loading. We had tarps on the truck to cover the sides, and we filled the truck to capacity. Lord only knows how many cans we had. Fully loaded, we headed to the convoy check point. When we got there, we were told there was no convoy going out today. That meant another night in Da Nang.

I left the driver and my two helpers to guard the truck. They slept on top of the beer! I am sure they drank their fill. I went back to the Army club and to my old platoon sergeant. The next day, I made sure we joined the convoy. The convoy would, after dropping the beer truck off at the battalion area, continue on to Dong Ha, and that's where I wanted to go.

Once at Dong Ha, I made my way over to the 12th Marine headquarters and reported in. It was dark and they put me up in a tent for the night. I was tired and quickly fell asleep. In the morning I checked back and was assigned to the FSCC (Fire Support Control Center).

As an old infantryman, I didn't even know what the FSCC was. They told me where their bunker was and told me to check in with Major Gray, who, by the way, would go on to become commandant of the Marine Corps. The major was a tough-looking Marine who asked if I had ever worked in the FSCC before. When I told him no, he said, "Well Gunny, here's the plan. Starting this evening, Gunnery Sergeant B. will be sitting at that desk, and you will be by his side from 1900 to 0700 in the morning. In two weeks, Gunnery Sergeant B goes home and you will be sitting at that desk alone, as the new operations chief. Any questions?

Starting that evening, I sat in, listened, and made notes. The FSCC had control of all artillery in the northern part of South Vietnam. The desk the major was referring to was a long, wide table, half of which was operated by the Army, and the other half by the Marines. The table was covered with a map, with all artillery batteries marked on the map and a circle drawn from the battery out to the limits of the battery's range. Looking at the map,one could see a series of circles, covering almost every inch of the map.

All patrol routes were plotted on the map, and if a patrol got ambushed or ran into any trouble and needed support, they were to radio the FSCC their coordinates. By looking at the map, we would know which battery (of the ones not in use) could reach that patrol. We would then call that battery for a fire mission. There were four radio operators on duty in the bunker, along with an officer in charge and an operations chief for the Marines and the Army. I really didn't learn an awful lot that first night, except that when the shit hits the fan, the bunker is busy as hell.

As the days went on, I quickly picked up what my duties and responsibilities were, so that I would be ready when Gunnery Sergeant B. went home. This was an entirely new experience for me, and I enjoyed the hustle and bustle going on in the bunker during the night. Working all night wasn't bad.I started at 1900 and got off at 0700 the next morning. As soon as I was relieved, I headed to the mes shall for breakfast. Then it was off to get some sleep. It was usally 1400 or 1500 in the afternoon that I woke up and headed for the showers. At 1630, there was an early supper, then down to the club for a couple of Cokes and socializing, before heading for the bunker at 1900 hours. At about midnight every night, you go over to the mess hall and pick up some sandwiches and coffee or milk.

The Army OP chief and I became good friends. I called him "the general" because the Army officers always wear all kinds of shiny things all over their uniforms, even utilities. He wanted to be a helicopter pilot and had applied for the position. If accepted, he would finish out his tour, and upon returning to the States, go to school for helicopters pilots.

One night when it was particularly quiet, he and I were fooling around with the maps on our desks. All these maps were covered with clear plastic, so you could plot on the map and then remove the markings when finished. On his map, he plotted moving this unit here and that unit there, and air assault over here, and Naval gunfire over there. It was all in fun, and we laughed about his strategy.

At 0700 in the morning, a young Army second lieutenant, new in the country, relieved the general and went over to the mess hall to eat breakfast. We had just sat down when the general was recalled back to the bunker on the double. "What the hell does he want now?" the general said as went out the door. A few minutes later he returned and was laughing. It seemed that he had forgot to clear his map of all the markings that he had made during the night. The new second lieutenant was all shook up because he didn't know what was going on!

Major G. was on his way up the Marine Corp ladder. He was promoted to lieutenant. colonel and was moving to Gio Linh, near the DMZ. Lieutenant Colonel G. would go on with his career to become the Commandant of the Marine Corps. Before he left, he asked me if I wanted to change my MOS from Infantry to Artillery. I told him I would think about it. He said there was an opening for an operation chief in the FSCC at Phu Bia, and it was mine if I wanted it. Phu Bia was the location of the Division FSCC.. I took the job.

Phu Bia was located outside of the city of Hue. When checking in at Phu Bia, the sergeant major told me that I would have to be billeted with the 12th Marines because that was the unit I belonged to. I told him that the 12 Marines were located at Dong Ha and that I was assigned to the FSCC here at Phu Bia. There would be no way to commute!

The tents here in the division were best yet. They were almost like the ones at Stateside, except for an occasional rocket attack. The food was better and the FSCC bunker was bigger and stronger than the one we had at Dong Ha. We used to say that an atomic bomb could hit the bunker and it wouldn't cave in. The tent area was about 200 to 300 yards away from the FSCC bunker. Next to each tent there was a sandbagged hole in case of an attack. When I worked at night, I was in the bunker, and during attacks, I was pretty safe.

The FSCC bunker was set up a little different from the Dong Ha bunker. There was a huge U-shaped desk sitting about two feet off the deck. The open end of the U was facing the wall map. Around the table sat a Navy officer for Naval gunfire, then a Marine pilot for air support, an artillery officer, an operations chief, and the officer of the day in charge. We also had six radio operators on duty. A Major W. ran the shop.

Every evening before dark, I was given a list of coordinates of the patrols going out that night, along with the coordinates of the areas to be bombed. Once I plotted all the patrols, I then marked the bomb areas. If a bomb area was in or near a patrol, I would cancel the bomb run on that coordinate.

One evening after plotting in all the patrols, I started in with the bomb locations. I couldn't believe my eyes! One of the coordinates to be bombed that night was our headquarters at Phi Bia! Needless to say, that was the first coordinate canceled.

Major W. came to me one night and said, "I want you to personally plot these locations on this map and don't tell anyone what you are doing." I took one look at the map he had given me and told him these locations were in Cambodia. He said, "I don't know what you are talking about. Just plot!" Who said we didn't shoot into Cambodia when the VC ran there.

The routine here at Phu Bia was the same as in Dong Ha: work 1900 to 0700 the next morning, eat breakfast, get some sleep till 1400 or 1500, hit the showers, eat an early supper, a quick stop at the club, and off to the bunker. The stop at the club here was better because they had a movie every day. I got to see a little each time but never the whole movie. I didn't mind.

I was coming out of the club one evening and heading for the bunker when all of a sudden incoming rockets exploded in the compound. I had to cross a wide open field of about 200 to 300 yards to get to the bunker. I took off running and when I heard more incoming explosions, I hit the deck. I still had a long distance to go and as soon as the last round hit, I was off and running again. I didn't know I could run that fast!

Once inside the bunker, things were happening. The pilot was on the radio for air, the Navy lieutenant had Naval gunfire on hold, the artillery officer had the batteries standing by, and a company of Marine infantry was waiting to lift off in helicopters to silence the intruders. Into the bunker came the commanding general of the area. He asked what we had been doing, what we had going. By this time, we had a compass reading of the location of the rockets, and all we needed was a signal to GO! When we plotted the location on the map, to no one's surprise, the location was in the yellow zone.

The yellow zone is a civilian area, which we could not fire into without permission of the South Vietnamese government in Saigon. By the time that permission was given, it was too late. The VC had moved on. The VC often fired from inside a civilian area, knowing we couldn't shoot back without permission. But we would, as soon as permission was given, lift the Marine infantry that was standing by in that area, with the usual results. The only evidence they would find is that we were there, but that's it. It was like Korea. Civilians ran the war and the people fighting the war were just pawns in the big picture.

One night a series of explosions was going off and inside the bunker. We thought, *Here it comes again.* The explosions kept coming but we could not figure out where they were coming from. Everyone was calling us, asking what was going on. Finally the word filtered in that the ammo bunker was exploding. Well, I mean to tell you that it was just like our national anthem, with rockets' red glare and bombs bursting in air. The explosions continued for over an hour; it was quite a show!

You learn very quickly to distinguish between incoming and outgoing rounds. It's really funny because you could be sound asleep in the middle of the night with our artillery going off all night, and you would never wake up, but with one round of incoming artillery, you were up and ready, just like that.

All newcomers arriving in Vietnam go through a learning process. First, you have to get over the dysentery because you will get diarrhea that will last about a week. Then you must learn to distinguish between incoming and outgoing artillery fire. If you don't, you will spend a lot of time diving to the ground. In the beginning, you look around when you hear the shells flying overhead to see how everyone else reacts. The instinct to get down is pretty strong, and when you're new, you go down most of the time.

One evening they were playing a Dean Martin movie, one in which he was a private eye (named Matt Helm, I think). Anyway, in the movie, all the buttons on his jacket could be pulled off and thrown as explosives. The whistling sound they made when thrown had many Marines flying to the ground during the movie. It gave the old salts a good laugh.

You never think of big brass getting killed or wounded, but in Vietnam, in 1967, a Marine Corps general on a routine helicopter tour of the area was shot down and killed. You see, the problem in Vietnam was that there was no way of telling exactly where enemy territory ended and our territory began. The enemy was everywhere and you could not tell the difference between him and your own kind. A sniper could be anywhere. I remember stopping on the side of a bridge. Four of us got out of the jeep and walked down to the water's edge. It was in the middle of the summer and hot. We decided to jump in (or, I should say *they* decided, not me). I am not a good swimmer and never went to the beach, so I sat on the edge of the water while they others went in. No sooner were they in when three shots rang out, as a sniper tried to make his quota. We were in the Jeep and on our way before you could say "Jack Robinson."

In Vietnam, getting the supplies you need was very difficult. In the FSCC, Major W. said he wanted me to go to Okinawa and pick up some of the supplies we needed but couldn't get. My going to Okinawa was all being kept quiet because it was done without any orders. In the FSCC, we had a Marine pilot who made the arrangements to get me on a flight to Okinawa and back. I went with a shopping list in hand.

In Okinawa, I ran into my nephew, Bucky. He was a Marine corporal and working in supply. I gave him the list and asked him to see what he could do. He knew his way around supply and how things typically got done. Before you knew it, I had my supplies and was on my way back to Vietnam. I received all the credit for getting the supplies, but it was my nephew Bucky, with his knowledge of the supply system, who did all the work.

When you become a short-timer in Vietnam, you look at things differently. I met an old friend of mine in Vietnam, who had been with me in California when we formed up the new Battalion. He had been promoted to gunnery sergeant while he was in Vietnam.

We had not seen each other since we got into the country. Now we were both short-timers. He told me that every night during the last week in the country, he had gone to sleep in the bunker right outside his tent. I don't know if he really did that or not, but with a week to go before you go home, you are pretty cautious about what you do and where you go.

In my last week in Vietnam, the major asked me if I wanted to take a helicopter ride out to one of the ships in the harbor with him. I thought, *Why not? We will probably get a good meal out there.* The Navy eats well. The next morning as we were preparing to go to the helicopter pad, he told me, "You know that there is no landing pad on this ship. We will have to be lowered down in a basket seat!"

"Major!" I said. "I am a short-timer and you want me to be lowered down in a basket seat from a helicopter and then lifted back up? A month ago I would have said okay, but now...no thanks." My lunch that day was not as good as I thought it was going to be, but it was a whole lot safer.

A gunnery sergeant reported in and had been sitting with me for over a week now, getting ready to assume my duties. At the same time, Captain H., an artillery officer, was waiting for his replacement. When his replacement arrived, the captain said, "Gunny, let's you and I go to the major and see if we can leave now! The major said you guys have no orders." We convinced the major that we could get orders once we were in Okinawa. With his approval, we started packing up. The captain called me aside and told me he wanted to take a carbine rifle home. He told me that he was breaking it down so it would fit easily into two bags. They never would check the officers' and staff NCOs' bags, so I agreed to help him.

Out to the airstrip we went and talked our way into being allowed to hop a ride to Da Nang. Once in Dan Nang, we made our way to the flight control center to find out our chances of getting on an Okinawa flight. They told us that officers and staff NCOs without orders could get on a flight if there was room aboard. All personnel with orders were seated first. We grabbed a cup of coffee and settled down in a corner of the waiting area, expecting a long wait. All of a sudden, over the loud speaker we heard, "Will Captain H. and Gunnery Sergeant Landry report to the counter immediately?" We dropped our coffee and ran. At the counter, they said a plane is getting ready to depart for Okinawa and there are two seats available if you want them. As we boarded the plane, they closed the door and headed down the runway. We settled down in the bucket seats and tried to relax. It wasn't a luxury civilian jet, but it had wings and it could fly. As we lifted off, we looked down and bid farewell to Vietnam!

CAMP PENDLETON
1967 - 1968

It only took a couple of days to get orders once we arrived in Okinawa. My orders read, "Camp Pendleton, CA." When I deployed to Vietnam, Masako and the kids remained at the government housing called Wire Mountain in Camp Pendleton. The plane leaving Okinawa for the United States was full. I remember thinking as I looked around the plane, *Every One of us has a story to tell about his experiences.*

It was a long flight and finally the words we all wanted to hear came over the intercom: "PREPARE FOR LANDING!" We landed at Travis Air Force Base in Fairfield, California, at 0300 in the morning. As we exited the plane, everyone made a beeline to the telephones. I called Masako. It was great to hear her voice again. I told her that I was taking a bus to San Francisco Airport and that I would catch the first plane out to San Diego.

My parents were at the house with Masako. Later they told me that after I called, Masako said she had to make a chocolate cake because she promised me she would make one when I came home. It was three in the morning and she baked a cake!

At the San Francisco terminal, everyone was just milling around waiting for his/her plane. San Diego is about an hour away from Camp Pendleton. There were four of us heading to Camp Pendleton, so we agreed to take a cab from the San Diego Airport to Camp Pendleton. The cab dropped me at my door and the reunion was great. Masako and the kids were the most beautiful sight I had seen in 13 months.

After coming back from Vietnam, everyone gets 30 days leave. During those days we became a family again and it was great. We went everywhere and saw everything. But we knew that one day I would have to report in. After 17 years in the Corps, I still looked forward to my next assignment.

Next I was assigned to an infantry battalion. I reported into the battalion and was sent to a rifle company as the company gunny. The company gunny is the senior enlisted man in the field, and he controlled all the training and field work, reporting directly to the company commander. The company was made up of mostly recruits, right out of boot camp. Only a few of the NCOs in the company had Vietnam experience. The officers in the company were inexperienced also, with only the company commander having been to Vietnam. The captain called for a meeting with all the officers and me. At the meeting, he introduced me to them and then said, "When Gunny Landry speak,s it's me talking." Things went well for a couple of months, then all hell broke loose!

The area in Camp Pendleton where our battalion was, had been completely sealed off by the military police. No one was allowed in or out. Rumors were flying all over the place. A meeting was called for all officers and staff NCOs in the mess hall. The battalion was ordered to prepare for deployment to Vietnam in 96 hours!

All enlisted men who had been back from Vietnam less than six months would not be required to go. All officers and staff NCOs would go regardless of when they came back. No one was allowed to leave the camp for any reason. I called Masako and told her the bad news. I told her I would call as soon as I heard anything, that they had a meeting scheduled for officers and staff NCOs.

Moving a battalion out in 96 hours is a tremendous task Every minute of every day, someone new reported in for duty. By the middle of the third day, we started loading the troops up, sending them to El Toro Marine Air Station. New word trickled down that officers and staff NCOs who had been back from Vietnam less than 6 months did not have to go. They added, however, that if we wished to go, we could. Yeah, right!

So I still no time off and was still not allowed to go home. We were living on the base but could not leave the battalion area. When the word came that the staff NCOs didn't have to go back to Vietnam, I called Masako and gave her the good news. I told her I would call as soon as I had any more information.

It was the beginning of the fourth day "home" and the battalion was a mess. There were people still checking in, getting assigned to a company, being issued all their gear, and then, finally, off they went. My company had not yet moved out. There was no replacement for me yet and the clock was still ticking.

I happened to be at battalion headquarters when a gunnery sergeant reported in to the battalion. I heard the battalion adjutant say, "You are going to Bravo Company." It was music to my ears. I told the adjutant I would show him the way. I took him down to the company, introduced him to the new company commander and to the three platoon sergeants, just in time as the word came down. "Bravo Company, move out!" My company commander, who also stayed behind, said, "Go on home, Gunny. See you tomorrow."

In the morning I went back to the battalion area and it was a mess. There were about fifty members of the battalion still there, and our job was now to get this area cleaned up. It took a couple of days. With the area now secured we all waited for assignment to new units. I was assigned to a new battalion in a different area of Camp Pendleton. When I reported, the battalion adjutant, seeing my record, told me that their existing operations chief was a short-timer and that they were assigning me to a rifle company as the gunny until his departure. Just a few more months playing Marine!

This new battalion was very much like the one that I just left. There were a lot of new Marines with little or no training, and inexperienced officers. I wondered when this battalion would be moving out. The company commander was a newly promoted captain and this was his first command. I talked with all the platoon sergeants and told them what I expected. For a while it was routine garrison work: formations, close order drill, and classes.

One of the platoon sergeants came to me about a private being the main cause of problems in his platoon. He asked if I could put him in another platoon—he had had it with this kid. I called the young Marine in and sat him down. We had a long talk. He was a tough kid from Chicago. He was pissed off because he wanted to go to Vietnam but nobody listened. That was my story 17 years ago, when I wanted to go to Korea.

111

I told the kid I would do all I could to get him to Vietnam but in the meantime he must do everything he could to be a Marine! I told him he now worked for me. "Just do whatever I tell you to do."

The captain called me in and told me that the company driver went out with the battalion that deployed to Vietnam. I told him I would take care of it. I took the private down to the motor pool and told them I wanted this Marine to get a military driver's license. He became the new company driver. I told him his duties included anything I wanted done. When the company went to the field they took their Jeep and trailer with them, and when we went to the field I didn't want to eat c-rations. I told him, "Your job is get food from the mess hall. I don't want to know how you get it. Just get it." I told him, "Make sure you pack the company tent in the trailer with a couple of cots."

It was supposed to be one week in the field. The trucks drove us out to the training area where we bedded down to get a good night's sleep before kicking off the exercise in the morning. With the troops deployed and security set, the troops pitched their pup tents. I had each platoon sergeant send a man over to the CP to assist the driver in pitching the company tent. With the tent and the cots set up, I asked the driver, "What's for dinner?"

The captain, when he saw the tent, complained that none of the other company commanders brought their tents out to the field. I told the captain that the reason the Marine Corps gives a company a tent is for them to use it, not leave it in storage. I told him it only takes a few minutes to pitch it and tear it down. And besides, sleeping on a cot is more comfortable than sleeping on the ground.

The driver brought in the Coleman lantern for light and the food for dinner. We had bread, ham, cheese, chicken, tomatoes, all the condiments you wanted, and a good cup of coffee. For desert we had cake. C-rations were never like this. The driver did good! The captain, sitting on the edge of his cot, said, "Gunny, where did all this come from?" I told the captain, "Just eat and don't ask." As we were drinking a second cup of coffee the battalion commander a lieutenant. colonel came in the tent. "All the comforts of home," he told the captain as he sat down with a cup of coffee. He talked about the next day and the mission of the battalion and wished the captain good luck. On his way out he added, "You were smart to bring the company tent. None of the others did. Goodnight!"

The exercise went well. Back in garrison, routine set in and every week people were pulled out and sent to Vietnam. When my driver got his orders he thanked me. I told him I had nothing to do with it and wished him good luck. I never knew what happened to him.

The S3 called me and told me that I was now transferred to H&S Company as the new S3 operations chief. I thought back to Gunnery Sergeant N., who taught me all about how to run an S3 shop as operations chief. He was the one who opened up the doors for me.

Since coming to California, we had been using a real estate company to rent out our $99-down-and-$99-a-month pink house in Jacksonville, NC. We received a letter from them telling us that renting houses in NC had gone south. They said most of the Marines who were going to Vietnam left their families back home or took them to California, and that renting units was impossible. With no renter, we would have to pay the monthly payment every month. I could not afford to do that, so I talked to my company commander about putting in a request for transfer to Camp Lejeune, NC.

It took a couple of weeks but the answer came back—no! I wanted to know why. I was told that there was no need for a 0369 gunnery sergeant in Camp Lejeune. When I heard that I blew my top. I told the daptain I didn't accept that answer and I requested to speak to the battalion ommander, a lieutenant colonel. A week or two later, I was told to report to the battalion commander's office.

Standing at attention in front of the battalion commander, I explained my situation and complained that the Marine Corps' answer made no sense to me. He told me, "Gunny, you have a problem, but the Marine Corps has turned you down and there is nothing I can do." I told the battalion commander I didn't accept his answer and requested permission to speak to the regimental commander, a full colonel. Everybody tried to talk me out of it, but I insisted that I hadthe right to speak to the regimental commander. It took a little longer for my request to get to the regimental commander's office, but it finally came.

"Gunnery Sergeant Landry reporting as ordered, sir," I said as I stood at attention in front of the regimental commander. The colonel looked up and said, "What's the problem, Gunny?" I explained (in detail) that I could not accept Marine Corps Headquarters' answer about having no need for a 0369 gunnery sergeant in Camp Lejeune, NC, home of the second Marine division. He listened intensely without saying a word. He said that I had a problem but his hands were tied and that Marine Corps Headquarters gave their answer, that and the matter was closed. "Sir," I said, "I request permission to speak to the commanding general." He tried to talk me out of it but I refused his advice. He then told me that division headquarters would call me.

What he failed to tell me was that they would take their sweet time in calling me. I was patient and was not going to give up. During the period of waiting, my battalion commander and regimental commander both talked to me again and told me I should just drop it. I was going to the top and I was not about to drop it. Then one day the word came. It had been so long ago that I thought maybe they were just stalling. "Report to the commanding general's office at 0900 hours tomorrow morning."

I was waiting in the lounge when the sergeant major told me to report to the general. Standing at attention in front of the general's desk, I said "Gunnery Sergeant Landry reporting as ordered, sir." The general told me to stand at ease and asked "Now Gunny, what's your problem?" I explained in detail, finishing with "I can't for the life of me, sir ,understand how there can be no need for an 0369 gunnery sergeant in the second Marine division at Camp Lejeune, NC." He responded with, "I can't believe they told you that, Gunny. Wait outside with the sergeant major." Snapping to attention, I said, "Aye aye sir," took one step backwards, did an about face, and left the office.

About ten minutes later, the sergeant major told me to report back to the general. I stood at attention in front of the general after reporting in. The general said, "You have been transferred to the second marine division at Camp Lejeune, NC. Do you have any other problems, Gunny?" With a great big smile on my face, I said "No sir. Thank you sir." The general said, "You're dismissed, Gunny." I took a step backwards, did an about face, and left the office. The sergeant major shook my hand and said,, "Congratulations Gunny. It took awhile but you got what you wanted."

By the time I made my way back to the battalion, area the word about the transfer beat me there! I stopped at the S3 shop and the battalion commander came into the office and said, "Congratulations, Gunny. I got to hand it to you—you stuck to your guns." The message from Marine Corps Headquarters in Washington had already arrived at division headquarters, and the transfer message filtered down to battalion for issuing of the orders.

I called Masako and told her the good news. She was delighted. I called my real estate company in North Carolina and told them I would be coming, to prepare the house. I checked out of base housing, had the movers come in and pack up all our belongings, picked up my orders and travel pay, and it was good-bye Camp Pendleton, and hello Camp Lejeune. I am probably the only Marine who ever wanted to go to Camp Lejeune!

CAMP LEJEUNE
1968 - 1970 (4ᵀᴴ Tour)

Another drive across the country. We traveled 500 miles a day, stopping every night for food, a shower, and sleep. We were up and on the road at the crack of dawn. We drove a few hours before stopping for breakfast. Bbefore we knew it, there we were, turning down Cardinal Road in Jacksonville, NC, to our $99-down-and-$99-a-month, little pink house. We got a surprise when we got to the house. The real estate man said my father had called him and paid to have the house painted before we arrived.

I reported in for assignment and was assigned to headquarters battalion H&S Company. This assignment was unexpected, as I was an 0369 infantry unit leader, but when I checked in, I was sent to NCO leadership school as an nstructor. I couldn't believe it! With all the hollering about wanting to get back to Camp Lejeune, I thought for sure I would be sent to an infantry battalion. Now don't get me wrong—this assignment was better.

I reported to the school and talked to the officer in charge, a Major G. The major said that all instructors had to attend a "Technique of Instruction" course at the Navy school in Norfolk, VA. When there was an opening, I would go. He told me to take a few days to adapt to the flow of the school and the classes. He assigned me to the map reading section, with two assistants. I was the primary instructor, with my two assistants roving through the class.

I was responsible for the lesson plans and evaluating the students' answers on the final exam, to see if the questions were too easy or too hard. I was also responsible to update the test, submitting new questions to be used on the final test to a board of section heads. I was a member of the board when evaluating other sections' questions. The class size ranged between 60 to 70 Marine NCOs. The "Map Reading" course was 12 hours over 4 days.

Before a new instructor could conduct a class, he had to present an hour-long class to the NCO of the school and to the major. The subject could be any military topic. I gave my "audition" (so to speak) on the UCMJ (Uniform Code of Military Justice). I remember what I had been told many years ago about giving classes, when I was giving classes at the first infantry battalion for new recruits right out of boot camp: "Tell them what you are going to tell them, then tell them and then tell them what you told them." I passed.

After a few weeks had passed, there was an opening in the Technique of Instruction school in Norfolk, VA. The school was consisted of three weeks of giving lectures and being evaluated and graded on each lecture. There were 3-minute, 10-minute, 30-minutes lectures, and a final 1-hour lecture. You could talk on any military topic. You had to include all the rules that had been explained to us during the first three days, and you were graded accordingly.

On the first day at the school I looked around to find that I was the only Marine. All the rest of the 25-member class were in the Navy. During the morning lecture, the Navy chief giving the lecture stopped in the middle of his lecture and said that there was one person in this room that really didn't need this class. The reason he didn't need this class was because he had been trained that way. I was sitting in the back of the room thinking, *What the hell is he talking about?* when he said, "Isn't that right, Gunnery Sergeant Landry?" He continued, "As a matter of fact, Gunnery Sergeant Landry could come up to the podium and take over my lesson plan and teach this class." I was sinking down lower and lower in my seat. He said, "Come on up, Gunny. Come on up and take over the class." As I got up from my chair and started walking up to the front of the class room, with all eyes following my every step. I thought, *That rotten son of a bitch. Why is he putting me on the spot?*

As I got to the front of the class, the Navy chief moved away from the podium and said, "Follow the lesson plan, Gunny. Take over the class." I took a deep breath. I stepped up to the podium and stared at the lesson plan. The page was completely blacked out except for a little white box in the middle of the page that read, "Tell the class to go to lunch." I took a second or two and then said, "If I am going take over this class, then I say let's go to lunch." I got a standing ovation.

Every Friday we had an inspection by the commanding officer of the school, a lieutenant commander. On the first Friday we were there, the lieutenant commander asked me to come forward and act like the platoon sergeant. Not a problem. I moved to the front of the formation. When the inspection began, I led the lieutenant commander through the ranks. I was shocked to see the condition of the Navy personnel. They needed haircuts, their shoes were not shined, their uniforms were dirty, and many needed a clean shave. At the conclusion of the inspection, the lieutenant commander raised the roof and I felt like a jerk standing in front of the formation.

When the lieutenant commander told me to dismiss the formation, I saluted, said, "Aye aye, sir," did an about face, and lit into these people. I told them I had never been so embarrassed in my life. This would *not* happen again. I told them that I didn't know the school rules or who the base commander was, but if anyone failed the inspection next Friday, they would be given duty all weekend. If I had to I would go to the base commander to get his permission. Inside the classroom, one of the Navy chiefs came up to me and said, "Gunny, pretty soon you will have *us* marching to class!"

The classes went on and the inspections on Friday were 100% better. Before we went outside for the inspections, students would come up to me and ask, "How do I look, Gunny?" After each inspection, the lieutenant commander said, "Good looking class, Gunny." I thought back to when I was stationed at Marine barracks in Sasebo, Japan. On that base, once a month the base commander—a Navy captain—would hold an inspection of Naval personnel and a platoon of Marines. They used to publish a monthly newsletter with the commanding officer's comments on the inspection. I was there for three years and I don't remember a month going by when the newsletter didn't say, "And the Marines, *again*, were the best."

In giving our classes, we were required to begin with a story related to the topic we were talking about. They said it didn't have to be truthful or real, just topic-related. I was giving a 30-minute lecture on the Marine Corps' LAW (portable rocket launcher used against tanks). I made up a story about my tour of duty in the Korean War, when we were under a heavy attack and I was sent with another Marine to protect our left flank from tanks. We took a LAW with us, moving down to where the tanks would come from. We sat in the foxhole for what seemed like hours as the attack became a full push by the Chinese. We heard the roar of the tank coming in our direction. The tank was blasting away with his machine gun, clearing everybody out of his way. We crouched way down in our foxhole, hoping and praying they didn't see us. If you fire a LAW at a tank from the front, side, or back, the LAW won't penetrate. But if you can hit the tank in the belly (bottom), you will stop it cold. In front of our position there was hole that the tank had to go through, and when the tank came up out of the hole, it would go way up in the air, its belly exposed. It was then that we would fire the LAW. We only hae one shot—ifwe missed the tank, it would come down and we would be dead.

We grabbed the LAW and as the tank came belly-up, we aimed and fired...nothing happened. We fired again and again nothing happened. The tank was coming down and we couldn't fire the LAW because neither of us knew how to remove the safety. I then went on to say this class is important because it could save your life.

After my lecture was over, we were on a break and I was getting a cup of coffee when one of the Navy members in the class came over to me and asked, "Gunny, what happened? You didn't finish the story...how did you get out of there?" I had made the whole thing up and this poor guy believed me! I wanted to say, "I died," just to see his reaction.

At the end of the school, they had a little graduation ceremony. They announced the top student...GySgt. Landry! I was surprised. I was called into the office and they congratulated me. They been looking for a Marine instructor and could get me transferred if I wanted the job, but I would have to extend my enlistment. I said thanks but no thanks.

Back at the NCO leadership school, the classes went on. Every month, another group would come in and the schedule would kick into gear. After my sixth group graduated, I was sent TAD to Viequez. I couldn't believe it. I had been to Viequez many times with infantry battalions, but this time I was going down there for three months as the base gunny. The reason for being assigned for only three months was because I was a short-timer in the Marine Corps. Yes, my 20 years were coming to a close. They have asked me about re-enlisting, but I have been stalling them. I was waiting to see if I was selected on the new promotion list that was due out any time now.

Viequez again. I flew into San Juan, Puerto Rico, and took a Navy shuttle ferry to the island. All the other times I had been here I came to the island as part of a battalion landing, whether it be amphibious or by helicopter. There was also a new base commander, a lieutenant colonel coming aboard. When I met the colonel, he told me that we were the only infantry Marines on the island, and together we would clean this camp up if we had to turn it upside down!

The first thing the colonel wanted done was to have the camp area policed up (cleaned up). All personnel, including officers and staff NCOs were to assemble at a certain time and then walk every inch of the camp, picking up everything that did not grow. I supervised the enlisted Marines and the colonel supervised the officers. There were a lot of disgruntled Marines on the island that day, but the camp was clean.

The next project was the troops. The colonel told me to take care of the enlisted and he would handle the officers. I don't know why the camp had been such a mess or why the troops looked like beach bums instead of Marines, but I put a stop to that. I started a morning formation and inspection of the troops and their quarters. I held a meeting of all the NCOs and explained what I wanted and what the uniform of the day was. This was the routine, Monday through Friday. I gave them some slack on the weekends. They began to look like Marines.

The colonel blew his top when he found out that everyone was using government vehicles for their personal use. He ordered all government vehicles turned in every evening at 1600 hours. No vehicles would be signed out on weekends unless authorized by the colonel himself. The only exception he made was his vehicle and my mine! In the staff quarters that evening and every evening after, I heard, "Hey, Gunny, when are you going to the club?"

The Marine Corps always had training classes, and even on Viequez, the training went on. I attended an NCO lecture and was shocked to hear how unprepared the NCO were and poorly they presented the material. None of the troops were even paying attention. I immediately set up an NCO school on the "Technique of Instruction," with me as the instructor. I held the classes three times a week, three hours per session. Within five weeks, the NCOs held training classes that were very well prepared and presented the material clearly so that the troops, believe it or not, actually learned something and enjoyed the session.

One big problem with the camp was dogs! They were running wild when the colonel and I took over the camp. Some of the troops even had dogs living in their barracks. The dogs were everywhere. The colonel told me to get "them damned dogs" out of my camp. We put a ban on dogs and I checked out a rifle to keep in my Jeep. Every time I saw a stray dog, I chased him with the Jeep, and as he ran into the hills, I took a pot shot at him. When the troops heard a shot, they used to say, "The Gunny is dog hunting again."

The promotion list came out and I was selected to the next grade, master sergeant E-8. My remaining time in the Corps was now very short, and I went back to Camp Lejeune NCO leadership school. The question was whether or not to extend my enlistment another two years. The sergeant major of battalion headquarters called me in and told me that he had my promotion on his desk, that all I had to do was pick it up and extend my time two more years. I asked the sergeant major where I would go if I extended. He said the Marine Corps base at Guantanamo Bay, Cuba! I told him no way. If I accepted that assignment (which was a six month tour as soon as I returned from Cuba), I would be going to Vietnam, which is a thirteen-month tour. In other words, if I extended for 24 months, I would spend 19 months away from home! He said they needed a master sergeant in Cuba and that I was it if I extended. I gave the sergeant major an optionJ: I would extend if they sent me to Vietnam, not Cuba. He said he would talk it over with the powers t be. In a day or so the answer was no. My next assignment would be Guantanamo Bay, Cuba. I refused the promotio

RETIREMENT

I was upset with the Marine Corps for dangling that promotion in front of me, trying to get me to extend for two more years. That promotion was earned for my performance over the last 3 and 1/2 years, not for future performance! But the Corps makes up the rules, and you either comply or get out. We decided to get out.

With the decision made, Masako and I had to now figure out what we were going to do and where we were going to live. I submitted an application to the California Department of Corrections and was accepted. I forgot what GS level they gave me, but I never followed up on it, because the Goodyear Tire and Rubber Company came on the base and started a new program called "Project Transition."

This program took the Marines who were getting out within the next month or two, and put them in a classroom for 30 days. Goodyear took a room the Marine Corps gave them to use as a classroom, and turned that room into the inside of an actual Goodyear store. It was identical, including the tire wall. There were a total of 20 Marines who signed up for the school. I was one of the 20. There were only two retired Marines in the class. The others were just Marines getting out after the expiration of their enlistment.

The instructor Goodyear sent to the project was an experienced Goodyear man for over 30 years. The way the program worked was that Goodyear was not required to hire you, nor were you required to work for Goodyear.

During the class, you could tell that some of the younger Marines were just glad to get away from their units for the month. For me it was a chance to get a job as soon as I was out. During the class, we read all of the printed material about Goodyear products. We learned the five steps to selling a tire, then practiced on each other. It was an interesting 30 days. At the conclusion, the director of personnel, from Akron, Ohio, came and interviewed each Marine. At the end of my interview, he offered me a job making more money than the Marine Corps was paying me, and I accepted. He then asked, "Where in the country would you like to work?" and "How long after you are out can you report?" I told him, "California," and, "30 days after release." It was done!

The ceremony for retirement was not a formal one. There were six of us and we assembled at the Camp Lejeune Field House. The officer in charge called your name, you stepped forward for your certificate of discharge, congratulations, and that was that. After 19 years, 6 months, and 28 days, I was a civilian. I have never figured out the reason for the extra 28 days. The Marine Corps credits you as serving 20 years upon completion of 19 years and 6 months. My 19 years and 6 months was up on January 27, 1970. The Marine Corps counts January as a full month, and that is considered my 19 and 6.

I had to wait to come home until I received my final pay check and travel pay on February 5th. Then I was told that you can't get discharged in the middle of the month, only on the last day of the month. I still don't know why, but that was their explanation.

I remained on active duty an extra 28 days. I actually was paid for doing nothing. I was completely checked out of my unit. The last 28 days were spent preparing for the movers and getting the car checked for another drive cross country to California via New York.

During the waiting period, I returned to the Goodyear School at Project Transition. I was in possession of a letter from the personnel director from Akron, Ohio, hiring me at an established salary and reporting me to the district manager in San Leandro, California. I was a little worried about what would happen when I reported in, as told, and the district manager says, "I am not going to hire this guy at this pay." The Goodyear instructor told me, "You see this signature at the bottom of your letter?" I nodded yes and he continued, "The only thing the district manager will say to you is welcome aboard.

After a quick visit to New York, we headed west to California. The trip was uneventful until we were outside of Springfield, Missouri. Our car broke down and we were towed to the closest garage. They told us that the parts needed to repair the car would take two weeks to get. I told them I couldn't wait two weeks. The tow truck driver said his cousin ran a small motel right there in town and he would be glad to drive us over there. On the way over to the motel he mentioned that his brother owned a used car lot, if we decided to buy another car. It seemed that he was related to everyone in town. What choice did we have? The next morning we bought a used Chevy Impala, and a rig, to pull out our service car, and off we went. I couldn't afford any more of his relatives.

In California, I checked in with Goodyear and was told to take some time to find a place to live. We wanted to purchase a new house. We stayed at the Holiday Inn in San Jose and went house hunting every day. Every new housing development had no houses for sale, just a waiting list. Almost discouraged, we stopped at a little place outside of San Jose called Milpitas.

When we talked to the salesman at the development he said he had one house available. We didn't hesitate. We said, "We will take it." The salesman said, "I'll show it to you," but I stopped him in his tracks when I told him that every thing we own is in the two cars out front, and that includes my wife and two kids. I told him we would take that house today, even if we hadn't seen it. He drew up some papers and we signed them. I told him we wanted to move in today. He told me that wasn't possible. He explained about the escrow, the new loan from the bank, the background check, employment history, and everything else that has to be done when purchasing a house. I repeated that we had to move in today. He called his boss and I explained that I wouldl put the rent money up front 'til the house closes. It took awhile but he agreed. We drove off to see the house we just bought for the first time.

He gave me directions and off we went. We went around and around and ended up back at the sales office. Red-faced, I went in and told them I couldn't find it. We followed his car and pulled into the driveway of our new home. Inside the house, we were both shocked by the color of the carpet. It was Spanish gold—that meant red! No wonder no one had purchased it! Civilian life had begun!

Printed in the United States
39871LVS00002B/145